...ge Broth
Crème Caramel au Riz
...sh Cutlets
Cheese Topped Veal with Butt...
...e Fillets of Beef
Continental R...
Fiesta Rice Dessert
Kalbsreisfleisch
Stuffed Tomatoes à la Grecque
...e Bisi
Salzburg Festival Lo...
Capsicum Cornucopia
Rice Custard Castle
Suppli al Telefono
Veal Oreg...
...mbalaya Lafitte
Oeufs à la Monteynard
...arrots
...uld
Pears with Cre...
Seafood Rice Salad
...e Rice Pilau
Poulet au Riz
Chicken...
Strawberry Rice Custard Parfai...
Marinara
Seafood Rice Curry Salad
Baked Stuffed Fish
Kedgeree
Meat and Rice Roll
Cheese Rice Soufflé
...rroz Verde
Chicken Supreme Rice Ring
Rice Lemon Lite
Rosy Apple Rice Dessert
Risotto con Scampi
Calabrese
Riz à l'Impératrice
Dolmádés
Col...
Sweet Curry
Larp
Soy Steak Supreme
Dolmas
...sienne
Huachinango Veracruzano
Arroz à la Catalan...
...and Cheese
Brown Rice Pilaff
Genoese Rice
Rhubarb Surprise Pie
Chicken Italiana with Olive-Cheese Sauce
Snowto...
Rich Fish Gumbo with Rice
Nasi Samin
Rice, Steak and Mushroom P...
...i Djuveč
Ham with Fruit Rice Dressing
Easter Bunny...
Creole Steak with Savoury Rice
Chicken Pilaff
Turkey Casserole
Pineapple Rice Salad
...dge
Pah Jook
Golden Rice Salad
...ng
Baked Rice Pudding
California Orange Rice with Seafo...
...ry Balls
Jet Rice Salad
Braised Chicken with Rice
...ghurt
Apricot Rice Meringue
Strawberry Parfait
Rice Salad
Rice Salad Nicoise
Pilaff à la Grecque
Veal with Rice Salad
Rice Topped Creole Cabbage
...rroz
Italian Green Rice
Brown Rice and Treacle ...
Grapefruit and Oni...
Peachy Rice Fluff
Crème Car...
...era
New Rice an...
Lemon Rice
Jambala...
Erdélyi Rakott Káp...
...cebake
...Rice Casserole

Great Rice Dishes of the World

Great Rice Dishes of the World

Trevor Wilson

URE SMITH · SYDNEY

First published in Australia 1970 by
Ure Smith Pty Ltd
155 Miller Street, North Sydney 2060

National Library of Australia Card
Number and ISBN 0 7254 0057 9
Library of Congress Catalog
Card Number 79-75372
Filmset in Monophoto Apollo by
Hartland & Hyde Filmsetting, Sydney
Designed in Australia
Printed in Japan by
Dai Nippon Printing Co Ltd

Reprinted 1971, 1972

Cover photograph by Paul Trenoweth

The author wishes to acknowledge the
generosity of the Rice Marketing Board of
New South Wales who made available all
their files of recipes and illustrations
and without whose help this book would
not have been possible.

Contents and Illustrations

Bold numbers indicate the pages on which the recipes appear.
Italic numbers indicate the pages on which illustrations appear.

Preface **xiii**

Introduction **xv**

Basic Methods of Cooking Rice

Fluffy Rice **1**
Pearly Rice **2**
Lemon Rice *(1)* **2**
Buttered Rice **2**
Creamy Rice *(2)* **2**
Fried Rice **3**
Riz aux Herbes (Herbed Rice) *(3)* **3**
Saffron Rice **3**

Rice Storage **4**

Western Rice Dishes

Austria

1 Salzburg Festival Loaf **8**
2 Kalbsreisfleisch (Braised Veal and Rice) **8**

France

3 Escalopes de Veau au Fromage *(9)* **8**
4 Sautéed Fish Cutlets with Rice *(10)* **10**
5 Poule-au-Pot **11**
6 Riz a l'Indienne **11**
7 Oeufs à la Monteynard **12**
8 Poulet au Riz *(12)* **12**
9 Poulet au Parisienne **12**
10 Gros Chou Farçi à la Provençale **14**
11 Chou Farçi à la Mode de Grasse **15**
12 Oeufs au Riz Bénédictine *(14)* **15**
13 Salade de Riz Niçoise **16**
14 Riz à la Dreux (Rice with Kidneys and Eggs) **16**
15 Rice and Salmon Salad Mould *(17)* **17**
16 Salade de Riz au Veau *(18)* **18**
17 Salade de Riz Méditerranéenne **18**
18 Salade de Riz Spéciale *(19)* **19**
19 Turkey à la Chevalière **20**
20 Chicken with Rice, Basque Style *(20)* **20**
21 Cheese Rice Soufflé *(23)* **22**
22 Strawberry Parfait *(13)* **22**
23 Rice Lemon Lite *(21)* **22**
24 Riz à L'Imperatrice **22**
25 Creamed Rice Soufflé *(25)* **24**
26 Crème Caramel au Riz *(24)* **24**
27 Crème Caramel au Riz (Alternative Recipe) **24**
28 Pommes au Riz Flambées *(27)* **26**
29 Peachy Rice Fluff *(26)* **26**

Germany

30 Bavarian Beef Crust Pie *(28)* **28**
31 Pears Pandora *(29)* **29**
32 Bee-Hive Bavarian **29**

Western Rice Dishes *(continued)*

Great Britain

33 Lattice Meat Pie *(30)* 30
34 Smoked Fish Kedgeree *(31)* 30
35 Rice, Steak and Mushroom Pie *(32)* 32
36 Meat and Rice Roll *(33)* 33
37 Cottage Broth *(34)* 34
38 Kedgeree 35
39 Cheese and Rice Mould *(35)* 35
40 Salmon Cheese Casserole *(37)* 36
41 Beef Carrots 36
42 Baked Stuffed Fish 36
43 Old English Rice Pudding 38
44 Brown Rice and Treacle Pudding *(38)* 38
45 Pears with Creamy Rice *(39)* 39
46 Loganberry Applebake *(40)* 40
47 Fiesta Rice Dessert *(41)* 41
48 Peachy Rice of the Ritz *(43)* 42
49 Rosy Apple Rice Dessert 42
50 Rice Custard Castle 42
51 Rhubarb Surprise Pie 44
52 Rice Biscuits 44
53 Strawberry Rice Custard Parfait *(45)* 44
54 Choco-Rum Baked Rice *(47)* 46
55 Apricot Rice Meringue *(49)* 46
56 Baked Rice Pudding 46

Greece

57 Avgolemono (Rice and Lemon Soup) 46
58 Dolmádés 48
59 Dolmas (Stuffed Cabbage) 48
60 Brown Rice Pilaff 50
61 Golden Rice Salad *(50)* 51
62 Chicken Pilaff 51
63 Rice à la Grecque 51
64 Pilaff à la Grecque *(53)* 52
65 Stuffed Tomatoes à la Grecque *(52)* 52
66 Capsicum Cornucopia *(55)* 54
67 Continental Rice Cake *(56)* 54

Holland

68 Dutch Oven Meat Balls with Chervil Rice 54
69 Dutch Rice Curry Casserole *(57)* 57
70 Dutch Curry and Rice Soup *(59)* 58
71 Stuffed Edam Cheese 58

Hungary

72 Czardaz Veal with Caraway Rice *(61)* 58
73 Erdélyi Rakott Káposzta (Transylvanian Layered Cabbage) 60
74 Letsho 60

Italy

75 Risotto con Uovi 62
76 Risotto alla Marinara 62
77 Braised Chicken with Rice 62
78 Prawn Calabrese *(63)* 63
79 Suppli al Telefono (Deep-fried Rice-and-Cheese Balls) *(65)* 64
80 Venetian Risotto 64
81 Chicken Liver Risotto 64
82 Risotto con Scampi 66
83 Risotto à la Norton *(67)* 66
84 Rice and Bacon Salad Bowl *(69)* 68
85 Risotto Milanese 68
86 Risi e Bisi 68
87 Riso al Limone (Boiled Rice with Lemon) *(70)* 70
88 Genoese Rice *(71)* 71
89 Mediterranean Cheese-Rice Salad *(73)* 72
90 Milanese Fillets of Beef 72
91 Veal Oregano 72
92 Chicken Italiana with Olive-Cheese Sauce *(74)* 74
93 Riso Primavera *(75)* 75
94 Rice Salad Supreme *(76 and 77)* 76
95 Chicken with Tuna Sauce and Rice 76
96 Italian Green Rice *(78)* 78
97 Osso Buco *(79)* 78

Western Rice Dishes *(continued)*

Portugal

98 Portuguese Risotto with Mushrooms 80

Russia

99 Russian Salmon *(83)* 80

Scandinavia Denmark

100 Danish Rice Pudding 80
101 Danish Almond Rice *(83)* 82

Scandinavia Sweden

102 Swedish Rice Porridge 82

South Africa

103 Sasaties 82

Spain

104 Paella à la Catalana *(85)* 84
105 Arroz à la Catalana 84
106 Salad Royale with Green Mayonnaise *(81)* 84
107 Suliman's Pilaff 86
108 Paella Barcelona *(87)* 86
109 Rice Barcelona 86
110 Paella *(88 and 89)* 88
111 Paella (Alternative Recipe) 88
112 Arroz con Pollo *(91)* 90
113 Arroz con Pollo (Alternative Recipe) 90
114 Stuffed Pimientos 90
115 Paella Espagñol *(93)* 92
116 Spanish Rice *(92)* 92
117 Spanish Chicken *(94)* 94
118 Paella Valenciana 94
119 Rice with Green Peppers and Cheese *(95)* 95

Yugoslavia

120 Sarma (Spicy Rice Stuffed Cabbage Leaves) *(97)* 96
121 Lovački Djuveč (Hunter's Stew) 96

American and West Indian Dishes

Brazil

122 Brazilian Rice 98

Cuba

123 Cuban Picadillo 98

Hawaii

124 Ham'n'Pineapple Quick Dish *(99)* 99
125 Hawaiian Rice Salad *(101)* 100
126 Pineapple Rice Salad *(100)* 100
127 Orange Rice with Bananas *(102)* 102
128 Banana Rice Fluff *(103)* 103
129 Rice and Banana Bake *(104)* 104

Mexico

130 Rice with Chilli Peppers and Cheese *(105)* 104
131 Crown of Rice with Avocado Sauce *(106)* 106
132 Rice with Fried Bananas *(107)* 107
133 Huachinango Veracruzano (Red Schnapper, Veracruz) 108
134 Red Mexican Rice 108
135 New Mexican Rice *(110)* 110

U.S.A.

136 Chicken Supreme Rice Ring *(111)* 111
137 Avocado Rice Salad *(109)* 112
138 Cheese and Tuna Rice *(113)* 112
139 Rich Fish Gumbo Louisiana 112
140 Rice Ring Rio Grande *(115)* 114
141 Rice Griddle Cakes *(114)* 114
142 Ham Rolls 116
143 California Olive Rice *(116)* 116
144 Jambalaya *(117)* 117

American and West Indian Dishes *(continued)*

U.S.A. *(continued)*

145 Seasoned Poultry with Rice *(118)* **118**
146 Lobster Newburg *(119)* **119**
147 Jambalaya Lafitte **120**
148 Baked Rice Crab *(120)* **120**
149 New Rice and Tomato Soup *(121)* **121**
150 Turkey with Oyster Rice Dressing *(122)* **122**
151 California Orange Rice with Seafood *(123)* **123**
152 Grapefruit and Onion Salad *(124)* **124**
153 Ham with Fruit Rice Dressing *(126)* **126**
154 Mexican Rice (Texas Style) *(127)* **127**
155 Jambalaya aux Ecrivisses à la Louisiane **127**
156 Salmon and Rice Casserole *(128)* **128**
157 Turkey Casserole *(130)* **130**
158 Seafood Rice Salad *(131)* **131**
159 Snowtop Peach Ricebake *(133)* **132**
160 Pineapple-Rice Alaska *(125)* **132**
161 Creamy Rice Meringue *(129)* **132**
162 Easter Bunny's Rice *(134)* **134**
163 Rice and Banana Cream Pie *(135)* **135**

West Indies

164 Colonial Rice *(136)* **136**
165 Creole Beef *(137)* **137**
166 Rice Topped Creole Cabbage *(138)* **138**
167 Pilau of Seafood and Rice *(139)* **139**
168 Pineapple Rice Pilau *(141)* **140**
169 Riñones en Jerez con Arroz (Sherried Kidneys with Rice) **140**
170 Tortilla de Arroz (Rice Omelet) **140**
171 Di-ri et Djon-djon (Rice and Mushrooms) **140**
172 Arroz Verde (Green Rice) *(142)* **142**
173 Creole Steak with Savoury Rice *(143)* **143**

Eastern Rice Dishes

Ceylon

174 Fish and Rice Kedgeree **146**
175 Chicken Pilau **146**
176 Ceylonese Curry *(147)* **146**

China

177 Tuna with Ginger Rice *(149)* **148**
178 Chicken and Almonds **148**
179 Kowloon Savoury Rice **148**
180 Yeong Jow Chow Fan (Yeong Jow Fried Rice) *(151)* **150**
181 Fried Rice with Eggs *(150)* **150**
182 Soy Steak Supreme *(153)* **152**
183 Sweet and Sour Pork *(153)* **152**
184 Heavenly Chicken with Rice *(157)* **152**
185 Canton Fried Rice **154**

India

186 Indian Chicken Curry *(155)* **154**
187 Devilled Grilled Spatchcocks with Simla Rice **156**
188 Marinated Beef Curry with Garden Rice **156**
189 Egg Curry **158**
190 Curry Balls **158**

Eastern Rice Dishes *(continued)*

India *(continued)*

191 Oriental Beef Curry and Rice 159
192 Sweet Curry *(160 and 161)* 162
193 Chicken Curry with Yoghurt *(163)* 162
194 Fruit Pork Curry and Rice 162
195 Rajah Chicken Curry with Golden Rice *(165)* 164
196 Seafood Rice Curry Salad *(176)* 164
197 Fried Rice with Prawns *(167)* 166
198 Prawn (or Egg) Curry with Lemon Rice 166
199 Kofta Curry with Cool Cucumber Rice *(169)* 168
200 Prawn Curry and Curried Rice *(181)* 168

Indonesia

201 Prawn Shaslik with Saffron Rice *(171)* 170
202 Nasi Gurih (Rice in Coconut) 170
203 Nasi Samin (Rice in Butter) 170
204 Nasi Kebuli Matrum 172
205 Nasi Goreng *(173)* 172
206 Nasi Goreng (Alternative Recipe) *(174)* 174
207 Nasi Briani Ikan (Rice with Fish) 175
208 Lemper (Rice Croquettes) 175

Korea

209 Pah Jook (Rice and Beans) 175

Middle East

210 Curried Pineapple Rice Kebabs *(177)* 176
211 Lamb Curry with Sweet Rice *(179)* 178
212 Sherkasiya (Circassian Chicken) 178

Pakistan

213 Beriane (Rice with Meat) 180

Syria

214 Syrian Chicken and Rice 180

Thailand

215 Larp 180

Preface

An eminent Chinese philosopher, one Lin Yutang, once said if a man is sensible he will count at the tips of his fingers how many things in life truly give him enjoyment. Invariably he will find food is the first one.

Secondly must come the choice of a food and the answer given by 70% of the human race is Rice.

Increasing numbers of people are eating more rice with the per capita consumption, particularly by non-Asiatics, rising in many countries.

In the United States of America consumption has risen over the past five years by 25%, and in Australia by nearly 20%. The United Kingdom and other European countries are finding rice as versatile a food as the USA and Australia have found for many years.

Gone is the day when rice was bought only as a cereal. Today rice has come to stay as perhaps the most versatile food that can be purchased.

All varieties of rice contain closely the same food value, and its recognition as the easiest of food to digest has been long established.

There are numerous other reasons why rice is so highly regarded as a food. The nutritive value of rice as compared with a few competing products shows the following:
Rice 86.09 per cent; Corn 82.97 per cent; Wheat 82.54; and Potatoes 23.24.

Rice can be served hot or cold, sweet, spicy, or savoury. It can be served as a breakfast dish, as a main dish, or a dessert. Rice makes an interesting salad, yet it is equally at home as a side dish with curry or meat. It is easy to store and prepare, because in Australia, it is packed and processed under the most modern and hygienic conditions.

The white grains of polished rice contain 79.1 per cent carbohydrates, which supply the body with energy. It contains 7.4 per cent protein, necessary for repairing tissues and building muscles. The protein in rice is specially valuable, because it contains amino acids that are more efficient in building and repairing body tissue than most other cereal grains. Under a microscope, rice has fine, thin-walled starch cells, and this is the reason why it is so quickly and readily digested. For this reason, nutrition experts have always recommended rice in diets for infants and growing children, and many manufacturers of baby foods enrich desserts and broths with this versatile cereal.

Rice is the most allergy-free of all the cereal grains, with an almost negligible fat content of 0.4 per cent. This, and its ready digestibility, makes it most valuable in certain diets.

Here is a book which proves beyond doubt how delicious rice dishes can be and offers the reader an international choice of menus.

It is commended for your happier and healthier enjoyment of living.

Charles E. Dalton,
Manager.
The Rice Marketing Board,
for the State of New South Wales

Introduction

This is a book featuring national dishes which require rice to be used as a constituent in the recipe rather than as an accompaniment.

All the usual types of rice are used, long-grain, medium-grain, short-grain and brown rice, and each of them has a place in the dishes which make up a Rice Cook's repertoire. Rice is the only whole grain and one of the very few basic ingredients which forms an indispensable part of such a wide range of dishes. Although it enjoys a traditional, symbolic and even religious role among Eastern peoples, its versatility has been much more fully exploited in Western kitchens. For this reason, you will see that the book devotes much more space to Western recipes, ranging right through the meal from soups to desserts.

The consumption of rice has been increasing considerably in the United States, the United Kingdom and Australia as its suitability as a universal accompaniment to main dishes has become more widely recognised.

In addition to the recipes in this book, you will discover several different ways of cooking the basic grain. All of them are correct, the different methods resulting in some variations in the finished dish, some in which the grains cling together, some in which the grains are separate. Each method has a place. Select the one which suits your kitchen and palate best.

The pictures are intended to help the reader to visualise what a dish will look like. As a good dish should delight the eye as well as the palate, it is hoped that this will overcome the problem which has exasperated so many readers of otherwise admirable recipe books. I have often found a list of ingredients so formidable and a method of cooking so ritualistic that, in the absence of an illustration, I can imagine that the ordinary reader could lose all capacity to visualise the finished product and be scared away from a dish that is well within her capacity to produce.

Trevor Wilson

Lemon Rice

Basic Methods of Cooking Rice

A number of national dishes are served with rice cooked in one of the many basic forms. Several of these recipes appear on this page and the following two pages. These are not numbered with the main list of recipes as they should not be regarded as complete dishes in themselves, but only as the rice section of a more elaborate main dish or dessert.

This list of basic recipes is by no means complete as there are dozens of minor variations using alternative spices such as caraway seeds or ginger. Several other variations appear in the main sections of the book, but have not been included in this section because they apply only to one recipe.

The principal characteristic of Fluffy Rice is that the grains remain separate; of Pearly Rice that the grains tend to cling together. Each has its place—Pearly Rice being identified mostly with Oriental dishes, Fluffy Rice with Western dishes.

Fluffy Rice

1 cup uncooked rice
8 cups boiling water
1 dessertspoon salt

Add the salt to the boiling water, then gradually add the rice. Boil rapidly, uncovered, for 12–15 minutes, then strain through a colander or large strainer, without rinsing. The rice dries out into 3 cups of large, white fluffy grains.

Pearly Rice

1 cup uncooked rice
water

Add water to 1″ above the rice in a saucepan, then boil rapidly with the lid off until steam holes appear in the rice. Lower the heat to lowest point, put the lid on firmly and leave for 20 minutes for the steam to complete the cooking. This will make 3 cups of Pearly Rice. This is the Chinese method.

Lemon Rice

3 cups ready-cooked rice
1 cup sugar
¼ pint water
grated rind and juice of 2 lemons

Boil the sugar, water, lemon rind and juice until the syrup is slightly thick. Add the rice, cover, and allow to simmer very gently for 50–60 minutes, stirring occasionally.

Buttered Rice

SERVES FOUR
8 oz. uncooked rice
½ lemon
1 egg
chopped chives
2 oz. butter
salt

Place the rice and lemon into a very large saucepan of boiling, salted water. Boil for 15 minutes, then drain and dry in an oven at moderate temperature for 2-3 minutes. Beat the egg and stir into the rice with the butter and a few chopped chives. Return to the oven for 5 minutes, then serve.

Creamy Rice

4 tablespoons uncooked rice
2 egg-yolks
3 tablespoons sugar
3½ cups milk
½ cup boiling water
1 tablespoon butter
vanilla essence

Cover the rice with boiling water and place over a low heat until the water has been absorbed. Add the milk and butter and continue to cook very slowly until the milk is almost all absorbed, stirring occasionally. Stir the vanilla essence, beaten egg-yolks and sugar into the rice.

May be served alone, topped with a dollop of cream.

Creamy Rice

Riz aux Herbes (Herbed Rice)

Fried Rice

SERVES FOUR

4 cups ready-cooked rice (cold)
3 eggs, slightly beaten
4 tablespoons diced shallots
4 tablespoons oil
3 dessertspoons soy sauce
salt
¼ teaspoon pepper

Thoroughly heat the rice in hot oil in a frying-pan or work over a moderate heat. Then thoroughly mix in the shallots, eggs and seasonings, stir and fry for 6 minutes. Remove from the heat and serve.

Prawns, diced barbecued pork, chicken pieces, beef strips, bamboo shoots or sliced mushrooms may be added to this dish with the seasonings to make a richer Fried Rice.

Riz aux Herbes (Herbed Rice)

1 cup uncooked rice
¼ cup chopped celery
¼ cup chopped onion
¼ cup chopped chives
4 cups chicken broth
¼ cup butter
½ teaspoon poultry seasoning
pinch of thyme
1 teaspoon salt

Wash the rice thoroughly. Melt the butter, then sauté the onions and celery until golden. Add the rice, salt and herbs and simmer slowly, covered, in the chicken broth until tender.

This rice preparation may be used for stuffing chicken or duck, or served with cold meats.

Saffron Rice

8 oz. uncooked rice
1 onion, chopped
2 cups chicken stock
1 oz. butter
pinch powdered saffron
pinch freshly-grated nutmeg
salt
freshly-ground black pepper

Melt the butter in a saucepan, add the onion and stir until it is transparent. Stir in the rice, then add the stock, salt, pepper, nutmeg and saffron (which has been blended with a little of the chicken stock). Simmer gently, covered, for 20–25 minutes.

Rice Storage

Where appropriate I have specified ready-cooked rice throughout this book, in the hope that readers will be encouraged to keep a stock of ready-cooked rice available at all times.

Rice is a very quick and convenient constituent of recipes, especially if you don't have to cook it when you are preparing the meal. Keeping it is no great problem, as cooked rice will remain without deterioration for quite a long time in a suitable container in the refrigerator. Tupperware, who have been good enough to provide me with the accompanying illustration, have produced a special Rice Container which keeps the contents in perfect condition.

I would recommend that long-grain rice be selected for pre-cooking as this is the grain most used where ready-cooked rice is specified. Short-grain rice, because of its greater absorbency, tends to be used in Paellas and Risottos, which require the rice to be cooked with the other ingredients. Long-grain rice is very suitable for Fluffy Rice, most widely used in any recipe that calls for white rice as an accompaniment.

Using one of the basic recipes printed on Pages 1 to 3, you simply cook the rice, let it cool, drain it thoroughly and place it in the Container, closing the lid securely. It will keep in the normal area of the refrigerator for days.

Western Rice Dishes

Western Rice Dishes

Rice may be associated in the minds of most people with Oriental dishes, but it took some folk genius of the Western world to discover that if you add raw rice to a casserole or rich stew, it will absorb all the liquids as it cooks. And in doing this it will become impregnated with all the flavours and aromas of the other ingredients. This discovery resulted in some of the world's finest national dishes—risottos, paellas, pilafs, dolmádés—coming from the countries bordering the Mediterranean. Of course the good news spread—to the West Indies, to Mexico, the southern United States, and Latin America. Today there are literally hundreds of variations on the basic themes. The possibilities are endless, but the basic formula remains the same. The meat, fish, or essential vegetable determines the character of the dish. This character is imparted to the rice, which acts as a vehicle to the flavours rather than a foil as in Eastern cooking.

Spanish dishes are possibly the most adventurous of all. There are no hide-bound rules for making Paella (its name derives from the dish in which it is cooked). It depends on the available ingredients, and each district contributes a variation for this reason. The result, at its most ambitious, can be an awe-inspiring combination of mussels, prawns, oysters, lobsters, snails, pork, chicken, chicken livers, saffron, onions, pimientos, tomatoes and garlic, providing a range of taste and aroma that defies description. Rice is the vehicle, the great combining medium, and perhaps the only common denominator of all Paellas. Almost all the other ingredients will change from district to district—perhaps enabling the trained gourmet to pinpoint the place of origin by its flavour as precisely as the dialect student could pick a man's birthplace by his speech.

It is important to remember that these provincial dishes—the paellas, risottos, pilafs—are not the creations of professional chefs or gourmets. In their own way they are an authentic folk art as surely as the folk song is.

These local recipes were seldom written down. You could not find them in cook books. Like other folk lore, they were handed down from mother to daughter. They were so fixed in the minds and hearts of the people that they could be recited with a certainty and precision unmatched by Escoffier. In gathering material for this book, I discovered an inexhaustible fund of information in the person of a Southern Italian woman who couldn't speak a word of English. From the rich store of her mind she could supply details of dozens of elaborate dishes with complicated lists of ingredients. All this had to be laboriously translated into English to enable me to use it.

The versatility of this remarkable grain extends its possibilities far beyond savoury or main-course dishes. There are wonderful desserts, ranging from the good old traditional Baked Rice Pudding to sophisticated French creations such as Riz à l'Impératrice. To round off the story, rice forms the basic ingredient for many delightful salads and cold dishes—particularly from the United States.

Not all the recipes in this section have their national title. Sometimes it has not been possible to find the correct national title, but where I felt certain of the original name I have included it. Some other minor adaptations are inevitable, for instance few people who read this book will have seen the original Spanish paella pot, let alone own one.

Where appropriate I have specified ready-cooked rice, but it is unsuitable for paellas and risottos because the character of the dish derives from the fact that the rice cooks with the rest of the ingredients. The only other thing to remember is that most of these district dishes are readily adaptable. Do not be discouraged if you do not have all the ingredients—alternatives may provide very acceptable variations.

Because of its superior absorbency, short or medium-grain rice is preferred for these dishes.

Stuffed Cabbage is a dish which appears in French, Italian, Greek, Spanish and Yugoslavian dishes, variously titled Sarma, Choux-Farci, Dolmas, etc. Variations on this dish feature the use of vine leaves, fig leaves or red cabbage leaves.

1 Salzburg Festival Loaf

AUSTRIA

1 cup ready-cooked rice
1 lb. minced beef
½ lb. minced veal
½ lb. minced lean pork
bacon slices
1 egg, beaten
¼ cup dried parsley
¼ teaspoon basil
salt
½ teaspoon freshly-ground black pepper

Combine all the ingredients (except the bacon) in a mixing-bowl and mix well. Line a 9¼″ pie-plate with aluminium foil and shape the meat mixture into an oval loaf. Place the loaf onto the foil, then cover with the bacon rashers. Bake in an oven at a moderate temperature for 1–1½ hours.

2 Kalbsreisfleisch (Braised Veal and Rice)

AUSTRIA

SERVES FOUR TO SIX
1 cup uncooked rice
2 lb. boneless veal, cut into 1½″ cubes
½ cup salt pork, cut into cubes
2 tablespoons grated parmesan cheese
1 cup finely-chopped onions
1 cup chicken stock
2 tablespoons lard
½ teaspoon sweet Hungarian paprika
1 teaspoon salt
freshly-ground black pepper

In a heavy saucepan, heat the lard over a high heat and add the salt pork. When the pork has browned on all sides, remove and drain it. Brown the veal in the lard over a medium heat, adding more lard as needed. As the veal cubes brown, transfer them to a 3-quart casserole and sprinkle with salt and pepper. Pour off all but a little fat from the saucepan and add the onions. Cook them, stirring frequently, until they are lightly coloured. Stir in the paprika, then add the chicken stock. Bring it to the boil, then pour the onions and stock over the veal and stir in the cubed salt pork.

Bring the casserole to the boil on top of the stove, cover tightly and bake for approximately 50 minutes. Stir in the rice, cover the casserole again and bake for approximately 25–30 minutes, until the rice is tender and has absorbed all the liquid. Stir with a fork once or twice during the cooking period, and add stock or water if the rice has absorbed all the liquid before it is tender.

Remove from the oven, stir in the cheese, and serve hot.

3 Escalopes de Veau au Fromage

FRANCE

SERVES SIX
4 cups Buttered Rice
(see recipe page 2)
6 thin pieces of veal steak
1 egg, beaten with 2 tablespoons milk
½ lb. cheddar cheese, sliced
2 tablespoons flour
1 can (10 oz.) tomato purée
3 oz. clarified butter
salt and pepper

Pound the meat to make cutlets as thin as possible, then cut into serving portions. Flour the meat and dip into the egg and breadcrumbs. Melt the clarified butter in a pan, then brown the meat slowly on both sides. Transfer to a casserole-dish, pour the tomato purée over and arrange the cheese slices on top. Bake in an oven with a moderate temperature (350°) for 15–20 minutes, until the cheese has melted.

Serve with the Buttered Rice

Escalopes de V
au From

4 Sautéed Fish Cutlets with Rice

FRANCE

SERVES SIX

2 cups ready-cooked rice
2 lb. schnapper or jewfish cutlets
1 ½ lb. tomatoes, peeled and sliced
3 onions, chopped
1 clove garlic, finely chopped
½ cup Sauternes
½ cup olive oil
chopped parsley
salt and pepper

Spread the boiled rice on the bottom of a large casserole. Heat the oil in a deep pan and fry the fish lightly on both sides. Remove the fish from the pan, and drain. Now fry the onion and the garlic in the oil until tender but not brown, add the tomatoes, salt and pepper and mix everything thoroughly. Remove the onions and tomatoes from the pan and spread them over the rice in the casserole. Add the wine to the remaining liquid. Place the fish cutlets on the tomato-and-onion layer and pour over the wine liquid. Sprinkle with salt and pepper. Cover the dish and cook in an oven at a moderate temperature for 15–20 minutes, until the fish is white and flaky.

Serve immediately, sprinkled with finely-chopped parsley and garnished with lemon slices.

5 Poule-au-Pot

FRANCE

SERVES SIX
1 stewing chicken (5-6 lb.)
1 veal knuckle, cut into 2″ pieces
2 onions, peeled and halved
1 leek (white part, plus 2″ green)
3 celery stalks, cut into 2″ chunks
vegetables (e.g. carrots, potatoes, parsnips, white turnips, leeks)
4 parsley sprigs
2 quarts hot chicken stock
2 quarts water
2 tablespoons butter
2 tablespoons vegetable oil
1 bay leaf
1 teaspoon salt
Stuffing

Wash the chicken thoroughly, then dry. Add the Stuffing to the bird, then close the opening with skewers and lace with string. (This keeps the bird in perfect shape while baking.) Melt the butter and oil over a moderately-high heat in a heavy saucepan, and brown the chicken in it lightly on all sides. Transfer the chicken to a 6–8 quart casserole and arrange the giblets, onions, celery, veal knuckle, leek, parsley and bay leaf around it. Pour in the chicken stock and water. If the liquid does not rise at least 2″ above the chicken, add more stock or water.

Simmer for 2½ hours, then remove the chicken to a plate. Strain the stock into a large saucepan, and skim off as much surface fat as possible. Discard the stewing vegetables, then return the chicken and stock to the casserole. Add the vegetables (carrots, parsnips, potatoes, white turnips, onions or leeks) to the chicken and stock, and simmer for approximately 30 minutes, until the vegetables are tender, then serve.

Stuffing
¾ cup uncooked rice
½ lb. fresh breakfast-type pork sausage meat
2 chicken livers
½ cup finely-chopped onions
4 tablespoons finely-chopped fresh parsley
¼ cup heavy cream
1½ cups hot chicken stock
2 tablespoons butter
½ teaspoon dried thyme crumbled
salt
freshly-ground black pepper

Melt the butter in a heavy saucepan over a moderate heat. Add the onions and brown lightly, stirring frequently, for approximately 8–10 minutes. Add the rice, and continue to cook for a further 2–3 minutes. Add 1½ cups hot chicken stock to the saucepan, then cover and simmer for 12–15 minutes, until the rice is tender and the liquid is absorbed. Put the rice into a dish and then, in the same saucepan, add a little oil and fry the sausage meat over a moderate heat until it is lightly browned. Drain the sausage meat and add it to the rice. Pour off all but 2 tablespoons of the fat from the sausage in the saucepan, then quickly sauté the chicken livers. Remove these from the pan and cut them into pieces. Stir them into the rice and sausage meat mixture together with the parsley, thyme and cream. Season with salt and pepper.

6 Riz a l'Indienne

FRANCE

SERVES FOUR TO SIX
1 cup uncooked rice
¼ cup toasted, slivered almonds
½ cup raisins
2 cups bouillon
2 tablespoons butter
½ teaspoon salt

Combine the rice, bouillon, butter, raisins and salt in a saucepan. Bring to the boil, and stir. Cover and simmer for 14 minutes. Add the almonds and mix lightly with a fork.

7 Oeufs à la Monteynard

FRANCE

½ lb. uncooked rice
4 eggs
4 tablespoons grated gruyère cheese
1 cup stock
1 oz. butter
salt and pepper

Boil the rice in the usual way (but for only 10 minutes), then drain it. Add the stock and simmer slowly.

Meanwhile, put the eggs into boiling water and allow them to boil for 5 minutes. Put them in cold water and then shell them. Butter an oven-proof dish and put in the rice (which should have absorbed all the stock and be quite cooked). With the back of a spoon, make 8 hollows in the rice, to hold the 8 half-eggs. Cut the eggs in half length-wise and put them into the places made for them. Season with a sprinkling of salt and pepper then add the grated cheese, putting a double-layer on each half-egg.

Pour the melted butter over the dish then place it in a hot oven for 3 minutes.

8 Poulet au Riz

FRANCE

SERVES FOUR
8 oz. uncooked rice
1 chicken
1 stick celery
1 carrot
1 onion (stuck with a clove)
1 clove garlic, crushed
cream
2 oz. butter
1 lemon
mixed herbs
1 sprig tarragon
salt and pepper

Put the butter inside the chicken, with salt, pepper, a piece of lemon peel and some of the tarragon. Rub the outside of the chicken with the juice of the lemon and a little salt. Put it into a deep pan with the onion, carrot and celery, and cover with water.

Cook the chicken over a medium heat, covered, for approximately 45 minutes. After 25 minutes of the cooking time, take out the carrot, onion and celery (and the neck and giblets if you have put them in) and put in the rice. Now let it cook fairly fast until the rice is tender.

Take out the chicken, cut it into 4 pieces, and keep it hot while you strain the rice. Have ready a large heated dish, into which you put the rice and on top of it place the chicken.

Heat the cream, but do not boil. Chop the remainder of the tarragon and add, with the crushed garlic. Pour over the chicken in the dish and serve immediately.

9 Poulet au Riz Parisienne

FRANCE

SERVES EIGHT
1 cup uncooked rice
1 chicken (5 lb.), cut into pieces
8 oz. small mushrooms (cèpes)
3 tomatoes, cut into quarters
1 medium onion, chopped
2 cups chicken broth
2 tablespoons olive oil
1 teaspoon salt
⅛ teaspoon white pepper

Brown the chicken in the oil, then add the broth and sufficient water to cover the chicken. Add the remaining ingredients and simmer for approximately 1–1½ hours, until the chicken is tender. The rice should have absorbed most of the liquid when cooked.

Strawberry Parfait (Recipe No. 22)

10 Gros Chou Farçi à la Provencale

FRANCE

Stuffing
1 large cabbage
carrots, sliced in rounds
shallots
onions, sliced
1 cup white wine
1 cup water
bay leaf
thyme
salt and pepper

Blanch the cabbage then remove the leaves, cutting off the hard stem. Fill each leaf with the Stuffing and wrap it up, tying it in place with thread. Place the wrapped leaves into a casserole with carrots, onions, garlic, shallots, thyme, bay leaf, salt and pepper. Pour over the white wine and water then cover the pan and simmer very slowly for 3–4 hours, moistening the top of the cabbage from time to time with its own juice.

Stuffing

2 cups ready-cooked rice
½ lb. beef, veal or chicken
meat from pork cutlet
1 sheep's brain
1 oz. lean bacon
2 eggs
2 oz. grated gruyère cheese
heart of cabbage, finely chopped
lettuce leaves
1 onion
1 clove garlic

Mix together all the ingredients (finely-chopped) and add the rice. Put the Stuffing into a pan with a little olive oil and allow it to cook for 1–2 minutes.

Oeufs au Riz Bénédictine (Opposite)

11 Chou Farçi à la Mode de Grasse

FRANCE

Stuffing
raw ham or bacon, diced
lean beef or veal, sliced
1 pig's trotter
1 large white cabbage
6 carrots
6 turnips
parsley
bay leaf
thyme
rosemary

Put the cabbage into boiling water for 5 minutes, then drain it and carefully remove the leaves. Spread each cabbage leaf with the Stuffing, laying them one on the other until you have used up all the leaves and Stuffing. Tie the cabbage up with tape.

Line a deep casserole with the slices of lean beef or veal, the ham or bacon, the pig's trotter, carrots, turnips and herbs. Put the cabbage in the centre, pour over a cup of stock (or water), cover the pan and cook extremely slowly in the oven for 2–3 hours.

Untie the cabbage, and serve it in the centre of a large dish, the meat and vegetables all round.

Stuffing

2 oz. uncooked rice
2 oz. pork or veal sausage meat
½ lb. minced pig's liver
3 oz. bacon
egg-yolks
½ lb. green peas
2 leeks (white part), finely chopped
heart of lettuce
1 clove garlic, crushed
nutmeg
mace
salt and pepper

Mix all the ingredients together in a large bowl and bind the Stuffing with the egg-yolks.

12 Oeufs au Riz Bénédictine

FRANCE

SERVES FOUR
3 cups ready-cooked rice (hot)
4 thin slices ham
4 eggs
1 tablespoon butter
Mustard Hollandaise Sauce

Brown the ham in the butter. While the ham is cooking, poach the eggs. For each serving, arrange a mound of the hot rice on the plate, top with a slice of ham, then top with a poached egg. Cover with a generous spoonful of Mustard Hollandaise Sauce.

Mustard Hollandaise Sauce

2 egg-yolks
2 tablespoons hot water
½ cup butter
1 tablespoon lemon juice
¾ teaspoon prepared mustard
salt
white pepper

Put half the butter into the top of a double-boiler, then add the egg-yolks and the lemon juice. Heat over hot, but not boiling, water. Stir until the butter is melted, add the remaining butter and stir until combined. Add the hot water and cook, stirring constantly, until thick. Remove from the heat. Season with the mustard, salt and pepper.

13 Salade de Riz Niçoise

FRANCE

4 cups ready-cooked rice
4 celery sticks, sliced
½ cup sliced cucumber
1 small tin anchovies
1 cup sliced radishes
3 tomatoes, cut into quarters
¼ cup sliced olives
1 cup watercress sprigs
lettuce cups
radish roses for garnish
Mona Lisa Dressing

Mix together the rice, watercress, sliced radishes, tomatoes, anchovies, olives, celery and cucumber, then chill. Pour the Mona Lisa Dressing over the salad, then toss lightly until well-blended. Place portions of the salad in the lettuce cups, arrange on a platter, and garnish with radish roses.

Serve as an accompaniment to cold meats.

Mona Lisa Dressing

1 cup mayonnaise
1 teaspoon horseradish
1 teaspoon paprika
1 teaspoon dry mustard

Mix together all the ingredients.

14 Riz à la Dreux (Rice with Kidneys and Eggs)

FRANCE

1½ cups uncooked rice
2 veal kidneys
8 eggs
1 tablespoon flour
¾ cup madeira wine
½ cup cream
3¾ cups chicken broth (strained)
8 tablespoons butter
pinch of nutmeg
salt and pepper

Wash, drain, and thoroughly dry the rice. Melt 3 tablespoons butter in a heavy saucepan over a low heat, then add the rice and stir until each grain is coated with butter. Reduce the heat and continue stirring for 10 minutes. Add 3 cups chicken broth, ½ teaspoon salt, ¼ teaspoon pepper, and cover the pan. Cook until small holes appear on the surface of the rice, then uncover the saucepan and put in a very slow oven to dry the rice. When practically dry, put the rice in a greased ring mould and tap down until it is firmly packed. Set aside to keep warm.

Cut the kidneys into very thin slices and cook them in a saucepan with 3 tablespoons butter. Brown lightly, and then add the flour. Mix well, then add the remaining chicken broth and the madeira. Bring to the boil and immediately reduce the heat. Add ¼ teaspoon salt, ⅛ teaspoon pepper, and the spice, then cover and allow to simmer for 10 minutes.

Whilst the kidneys are cooking, melt 2 tablespoons butter in a pan, add the eggs (lightly beaten) with salt and the cream. Heat slowly, stirring constantly. Do not over-cook.

To serve, unmould the rice ring onto a serving-dish, pile the scrambled eggs in the centre, and arrange the kidneys round the rice with their sauce poured over them.

15 Rice and Salmon Salad Mould

FRANCE

SERVES TWELVE

6 cups ready-cooked rice
1 can shredded salmon
12 hard-boiled eggs, chopped
2 cups diced celery
2 cups diced green pepper
1 cup diced pimiento
2 pints chicken stock
1 cup gelatine
2/3 cup mayonnaise
2/3 cup creamy french dressing
1/2 cup lemon juice
3 tablespoons salt

Dissolve the gelatine and add the chicken stock. Heat and stir until the gelatine is completely dissolved, then add the shredded salmon, green pepper, celery, pimiento, rice and hard-boiled eggs. Add the salt to the stock and gelatine, and mix well. Combine the lemon juice with the mayonnaise and french dressing, then add this to the mixture. Pour into moulds (or 1 large mould), chill, and allow to set until firm.

Serve with salad greens, tomato wedges, olives or radish garnish, or hard-boiled eggs.

16 Salade de Riz au Veau

FRANCE

SERVES FOUR

4 cups ready-cooked rice
veal
2 sticks celery, chopped
2 tomatoes, peeled and chopped
2 tablespoons chopped green capsicum
12 olives
2 oz. raisins, chopped
2 tablespoons white vinegar
2 tablespoons olive oil
1 teaspoon grated nutmeg
¼ teaspoon pepper

Heat the rice in a saucepan with the oil, vinegar, nutmeg, pepper, celery, olives (whole), tomatoes, raisins and capsicum, and mix well to thoroughly blend the flavours.

Serve with the veal, either hot or cold.

17 Salade de Riz Méditerranéenne

FRANCE

3 cups ready-cooked rice
chopped celery
tomato, peeled and sliced
red and green pimientos
black olives, stoned
tarragon vinegar
olive oil
fresh basil leaves
grated nutmeg
salt and black pepper

Put the ready-cooked rice in a salad bowl which has been wiped with a clove of garlic. Mix in some olive oil, tarragon vinegar, salt, black pepper and a very little grated nutmeg. Add the chopped celery, fresh basil leaves, tomato and red and green pimientos (cut into small pieces). Mix all the ingredients thoroughly through the rice and decorate the top with a few stoned black olives and slices of tomato. Chill for ½ hour before serving.

18 Salade de Riz Spéciale

FRANCE

1 ½ cups ready-cooked rice
1 ½ cups cottage cheese
endive or lettuce
3 shallots, chopped
1 dessertspoon chopped parsley
¼ cup french dressing
paprika
salt and pepper

Combine the shallots, parsley, rice, cottage cheese, french dressing, salt and pepper and mix thoroughly. Serve the salad in individual salad bowls lined with endive, and sprinkle with a little paprika.

Serve chilled with cold fish or meat, or by itself.

19 Turkey à la Chevalière

FRANCE

Buttered Rice (see recipe page 2)
12 oz. white turkey meat
small fillets of turkey (thigh and drumstick)
bacon rashers
3 egg-yolks
celery
1 onion
breadcrumbs
mushroom stalks
herbs

Make a stock from some of the turkey bones simmered with an onion, celery, herbs and mushroom stalks. This stock should be made into a sauce by thickening with the egg-yolks. Mince the white turkey meat and place in a small pan with sufficient of the sauce to bring it to the consistency of jam, warming gently over a low heat. Dip the fillets in the sauce, roll them in the breadcrumbs, and fry them golden-yellow in very hot fat.

To serve, put the mince inside a circle of hot Buttered Rice. Arrange the fillets on the outside, alternated with rolls of crisply fried bacon, and serve the remainder of the sauce, very hot, separately.

20 Chicken with Rice, Basque Style

FRANCE

1 cup uncooked rice
1 roasting chicken (medium size)
1 garlic sausage
1 lb. tomatoes, chopped
1 onion, sliced
3 capsicums
1 clove garlic
1 piece orange peel
bay leaf
½ teaspoon thyme
½ teaspoon marjoram
1 tablespoon paprika
salt and pepper

Brown the chicken (whole) in a large heavy saucepan in a little butter, together with the onion, thyme, bay leaf, salt and pepper. When it is golden all over, pour over enough warm water to just cover the bird, add the sausage (skinned) in one piece, and the orange peel, and simmer with the cover on until tender. This should take approximately 40 minutes.

Whilst the chicken is cooking, cut the peppers into strips, removing all the seeds. Sauté the peppers in a little butter and, when they are half-cooked, add the tomatoes, salt, pepper and marjoram. Turn down the heat and simmer until tender. Stir in a tablespoon of paprika, then set aside. Cook the rice in boiling, well-salted water for 12–15 minutes, until it is nearly tender. Drain it, and put it into a fairly deep oven-proof dish.

Take out the chicken and sausage. Pour 2–3 tablespoons of the stock over the rice and stir over a very gentle heat. When the rice has absorbed the stock, carve the chicken into suitable pieces for serving and place on top of the rice. Pour the tomato mixture over the chicken, and garnish with the sausage cut into cubes.

Rice Lemon
(Recipe No.

21 Cheese Rice Soufflé

FRANCE

SERVES FOUR TO SIX

2 cups ready-cooked rice
6 eggs, separated
1 cup shredded sharp processed cheese
1 can (10½ oz.) condensed cream of mushroom soup
2 tablespoons chopped shallot
1 tablespoon butter
¼ teaspoon curry powder

Cook the shallot and curry powder in butter until the shallot is tender. Blend in the soup and cheese and heat slowly until the cheese is melted. Beat the egg-yolks until they are thick and lemon-coloured, and stir into the soup mixture, then add the rice. Beat the egg-whites in a large bowl until they are stiff, then fold the soup mixture into the egg-whites. Pour into an ungreased 2-quart casserole. Bake in an oven (300°) for 1–1¼ hours, until the soufflé is golden brown. Serve immediately.

22 Strawberry Parfait

FRANCE

1½ cups ready-cooked rice
1 cup finely-sliced strawberries
½ cup sugar
½ cup white wine
1 cup whipped cream
1½ level tablespoons gelatine (dissolved in the wine)
2 tablespoons lemon juice

Mix together the strawberries, lemon juice, wine, sugar and gelatine, stirring the sugar until dissolved, then allow to set. Mix the rice and whipped cream in a bowl and sweeten to taste.

Alternate layers of rice and the set strawberries in parfait glasses. Top off with whipped cream, and garnish with a fresh strawberry and leaf.
(Illustration page 13).

23 Rice Lemon Lite

FRANCE

SERVES FOUR

3 cups ready-cooked rice
1 medium can sliced peaches or strawberries
1⁄1 cup desiccated coconut
1 can condensed milk
½ pint cream, whipped until stiff
rind of 1 lemon
6 tablespoons lemon juice

Combine the milk, rice, lemon juice and rind in a bowl. Blend and chill. Place alternate layers of Rice Lemon Lite, fruit, cream, and a sprinkling of coconut, into 4 parfait glasses (or individual dessert plates). Top with fresh or glacé cherries.
(Illustration page 21).

24 Riz à l'Impératrice

FRANCE

4 tablespoons uncooked rice
2 egg-yolks
1 cup fresh chopped fruit
½ pint jelly (orange or raspberry flavoured)
chopped mint
3 tablespoons sugar
3½ cups milk
1 tablespoon boiling water
½ cup boiling water
1 tablespoon butter
vanilla essence

Cover the rice with boiling water and place over a low heat until the water has been absorbed. Add the milk and butter and continue to cook very slowly, stirring occasionally, until the milk is almost all absorbed. Stir the vanilla essence, beaten egg-yolks and sugar into the rice. Mould into a lightly-oiled ring —leaving 1″ for the jelly mixture.

Make ½ pint orange or raspberry-flavoured jelly. Add 1 cup of fresh chopped fruit and a little chopped mint. Cool and pour on top of the rice. Leave to set, unmould, and decorate with pineapple rings cut in half. Serve with raspberry jam (thinned-down).

Cheese Rice Sou

25 Creamed Rice Soufflé

FRANCE

SERVES SIX

10 oz. Creamy Rice
(see recipe page 2)
2 egg-whites
¼ pint whipped cream
3 dessertspoons gelatine
3 tablespoons cold water
pinch of salt

Soften the gelatine in the cold water, and dissolve over boiling water. Beat the egg-whites and salt until stiff. Mix the dissolved gelatine through the Creamy Rice, fold in the egg-whites, then the cream. Fill the soufflé into individual sweet dishes, a large glass bowl, or a prepared soufflé dish. Chill until set. Decorate with whipped cream and chocolate shavings.

To prepare the soufflé dish—oil a straight-sided soufflé dish and, to give extra depth, tie a collar of oiled aluminium foil around the outside. Remove the foil before serving.

26 Crème Caramel au Riz

FRANCE

SERVES FOUR

1 cup uncooked rice
6 oz. sugar
4 oz. cream
1 pint milk
juice of 1 lemon
1 large piece of lemon peel
2 oz. candied peel, finely chopped

Put the milk in the top half of a double saucepan and put in the rice, 4 tablespoons sugar and the lemon peel. Cover the pan and simmer until the rice is cooked (approximately 1½–2 hours). The rice should have absorbed nearly all the milk and be very creamy. Turn the rice into a soufflé dish and mix in the lemon juice, the cream (which should be fairly thick) and the finely-chopped candied peel. Smooth the surface of the mixture and chill thoroughly.

Now spread on the top of the smooth surface of the rice a layer of sugar (¼″ thick). Have the grill already hot and put the dish underneath it, fairly close to the heat. In approximately 2 minutes the sugar will have turned to toffee on the top. Turn off the grill the second the sugar looks set, to avoid burning.

When cool, refrigerate the dish and serve very cold.

27 Crème Caramel au Riz (Alternative Recipe)

FRANCE

1½ cups ready-cooked rice
2 eggs
½ cup sugar
1 pint milk
2 tablespoons water
1 teaspoon lemon juice

Place the sugar, water and lemon juice in a small saucepan over a low heat. Stir until the sugar is dissolved, then allow to boil until the syrup is golden brown. Pour over the sides and base of an oven-proof dish, and allow to set. Beat the eggs and vanilla, then add the milk and cooked rice. Pour into the caramel-lined dish. Bake in an oven at moderate temperature until set.

Creamed Rice Sou

28 Pommes au Riz Flambées

FRANCE

3 cups Creamy Rice
(see recipe page 2)
2 egg-whites
2 oz. sugar
strawberry jam
4 oz. brandy
1 ½ cups sweetened apple purée

Place ⅓ of the Creamy Rice into a greased oven-proof dish. Cover with a thin layer of strawberry jam. Repeat this twice, and cover the top layer with the apple purée. To prepare the meringue, whip the egg-whites until stiff and gradually beat in the sugar. Pile the meringue on top of the apple. Bake in an oven at a moderate temperature for 20 minutes.

Warm the brandy and pour over the pudding. Set alight, and serve immediately.

29 Peachy Rice Fluff

FRANCE

3 cups Creamy Rice
(see recipe page 2)
2 egg-whites
1 large can sliced peaches (drained)
2 oz. sugar
½ cup coconut

To prepare the meringue, beat the egg-whites until stiff, then gradually add the sugar and beat well. Lightly fold the Creamy Rice and chopped fruit through the meringue. Place in an oven-proof dish and sprinkle with coconut. Bake in a slow to moderate-temperature oven for 35-40 minutes.

30 Bavarian Beef Crust Pie

GERMANY

SERVES SIX
Savoury Rice
1 lb. rissole steak
1 medium onion, chopped
1 tablespoon chopped parsley
½ cup breadcrumbs
3 tablespoons tomato sauce
pinch of mixed herbs
pinch of cayenne pepper
1 teaspoon salt

Combine the steak, breadcrumbs, parsley, tomato sauce, onion, herbs, salt and pepper to make the crust. Press the mixture onto the bottom and sides to line a 9" pie-plate. Bake in an oven at moderate temperature for 30 minutes. Remove from the oven and drain off any excess fat.

Spoon the Savoury Rice into the meat crust and sprinkle with the remainder of the cheese. Return to the oven and cook for a further 20 minutes.

Savoury Rice
⅔ cup uncooked rice
6 oz. shredded cheddar cheese
3 medium tomatoes, peeled and chopped
¼ cup chopped green pepper
pinch of cayenne pepper
½ teaspoon salt

Cook the rice in boiling, salted water for 12 minutes, adding the green pepper during the last 5 minutes of cooking time, then drain. Add the tomatoes, half the shredded cheddar cheese, the salt and cayenne pepper to the rice, and mix well.

31 Pears Pandora

GERMANY

½ cup uncooked rice
2 eggs, beaten
½ cup chopped glacé fruits
angelica
1 tin sweetened condensed milk
½ pint water

Place the rice in a saucepan, with water to ¾'' above the level of the rice. Cover with foil and replace the lid. Cook over a high heat for 3 minutes, lower the heat and cook for a further 9 minutes. Place the cooked rice in a double-boiler with the condensed milk and water and cook for ½ hour. Add the well-beaten eggs and cook for a further ½ hour. Add the chopped glacé fruits then spread on a platter to cool.

Divide the mixture into 6 equal portions and mould with hands into pear shapes. Egg-wash, bread crumb and deep-fry. Use angelica to form the stalks.

Serve on a bed of custard, hot or cold.

32 Bee-Hive Bavarian

GERMANY

½ cup uncooked rice
½ cup chopped glacé cherries
dates
halved blanched almonds
nuts
1 cup cream
1 tin sweetened condensed milk
1 tablespoon gelatine
1 teaspoon lemon juice
¼ teaspoon vanilla essence

Place the rice in a saucepan and cover with water to ¾'' above the level of the rice. Cover with foil and replace the lid. Cook over a high heat for 3 minutes, lower the heat and cook for a further 9 minutes. Place the cooked rice in a double-boiler with the condensed milk and ½ pint water, and cook for 1 hour. Add the lemon juice and vanilla essence and allow it to cool.

Soften the gelatine in 2 tablespoons of cold water, then dissolve in ¼ cup boiling water and stir into the rice mixture. Whip the cream, fold into the rice, then add the nuts and cherries. Turn into a buttered medium-size basin and chill for 4 hours. Un-mould and decorate.

To Make the Bees

A date forms the body—the wings are made from halved blanched almonds.

33 Lattice Meat Pie

GREAT BRITAIN

SERVES SIX

2 cups ready-cooked rice
1 lb. minced steak
$\frac{1}{4}$ lb. processed cheese
1 onion, minced
1 $\frac{3}{4}$ cups cheese cracker crumbs
1 cup tomato purée
$\frac{1}{4}$ cup very soft butter
1 tablespoon oil
$\frac{1}{4}$ teaspoon celery salt
1 teaspoon salt
$\frac{1}{8}$ teaspoon black pepper

Mix the butter, cracker crumbs and 3 tablespoons water together. Press the mixture over the bottom and sides of a greased deep pie-plate to make a crust, and bake in an oven at moderate temperature for 10 minutes.

Brown the onion and steak in oil in a heavy frying-pan. Cook until the meat is tender, then add the rice, salt, pepper, celery salt and $\frac{1}{2}$ cup water. Cook slowly, stirring, until the liquid is absorbed, then stir in the tomato purée. Pack the mixture into the crust. Cut the cheese into thin strips and place them across the top in a lattice design. Bake in an oven at moderate temperature for approximately 30 minutes, until the cheese browns and the meat and rice are hot.

34 Smoked Fish Kedgeree

GREAT BRITAIN

2 cups ready-cooked rice
1 lb. smoked haddock or cod
1 dessertspoon finely-chopped onion
$\frac{1}{4}$ cup finely-chopped red pepper (parboiled)
1 tablespoon finely-chopped parsley
3 cups white sauce
1 dessertspoon lemon juice
pinch of sweet basil
pinch of cayenne pepper

Cover the smoked fish with cold water and bring very slowly to the boil. Pour off the water and repeat the process. When the fish is tender, remove the skin and bones, and break it into small pieces. Place the pieces in a saucepan with all the other ingredients (except the rice), mix thoroughly and heat gently.

Serve in hot ramekin dishes, with a rice border.

Smoked Fish Kedgeree

35 Rice, Steak and Mushroom Pie

GREAT BRITAIN

SERVES FIVE TO SIX

½ cup uncooked rice
¾ lb. minced steak
¼ lb. mushrooms
flaky pastry (make with 8 oz. flour)
1 ½ cups meat or vegetable stock
½ teaspoon powdered thyme
salt and pepper

Place the rice, meat, mushrooms, stock, seasonings and herbs into a pan. Bring slowly to the boil, cover with a lid, reduce the heat and simmer gently for 30 minutes, until the liquid is absorbed. Transfer the mixture to a pie-dish and allow it to cool. Roll out the pastry, cut a narrow strip and place it round the edge of the dampened pie-dish. Cover the dish with the remainder of the pastry. Make several slits in the top and brush it over with glaze. Bake in a hot oven for 15–20 minutes, and serve immediately.

36 Meat and Rice Roll

GREAT BRITAIN

SERVES SIX TO EIGHT

1½ lb. beef steak
½ lb. veal steak
1 egg-yolk
1 onion, minced
½ cup soft breadcrumbs
dried breadcrumbs
1–2 tablespoons milk
¼ teaspoon oregano
salt and pepper

Filling

2 cups ready-cooked rice
½ lb. pork sausages
1 dessertspoon finely-chopped shallot
1 dessertspoon finely-chopped parsley
1 dessertspoon Worcestershire Sauce
salt

Mince the steaks and add the onion and seasonings, soft breadcrumbs, egg-yolk and enough milk to make into a smooth, firm mixture. Press the mixture out onto greaseproof paper to an oblong measuring 14″ x 10″. Spread the Filling over the meat, and roll up. Roll in the dried breadcrumbs, pressing them on to firm them. Wrap in greased aluminium foil and chill in the refrigerator for 2 hours. Heat the fry-pan to 360°–380° and place in the prepared, foil-wrapped roll, then cook for 5 minutes on all sides. Reduce the heat to 260°–300° and cook with the lid on for 1½–2 hours, turning frequently during cooking.

Serve hot, with baked vegetables, or cold with salads.

Filling

Combine all the ingredients.

37 Cottage Broth

GREAT BRITAIN

4 oz. uncooked rice
1 carrot, diced
½ turnip, diced
1 parsnip, diced
1 stalk celery, diced
1 onion, chopped
1 tablespoon chopped parsley
1 teaspoon sugar
4 pints beef stock
1 tablespoon butter
salt and pepper

Sauté the vegetables lightly in the butter. Add the stock, sugar, salt and rice. Bring to the boil then simmer gently for 1 hour. Season to taste with salt and pepper. Sprinkle with the chopped parsley before serving.

38 Kedgeree

GREAT BRITAIN

1 cup ready-cooked rice
cold fish
2 soft-boiled eggs
1 oz. butter
1 teaspoon mustard
cayenne
salt

Carefully remove the bones from the fish and mix it with the other ingredients in a saucepan. Cook for 20 minutes over a moderate heat.

Serve very hot.

39 Cheese and Rice Mould

GREAT BRITAIN

SERVES FOUR TO FIVE
1 cup ready-cooked rice
1 egg
1 cup shredded cheese
1 ½ cups raw shredded carrot
cooked green peas
1 small onion, finely chopped
2 teaspoons salt
½ teaspoon pepper

Cook the carrot for 5 minutes, then drain. Lightly mix in the rice, onion, well-beaten egg, cheese and seasonings. Turn into a prepared ring-mould, buttered and crumbed, and bake in an oven at moderate temperature for 30–40 minutes. Turn out onto a serving-dish and fill the centre with cooked, hot green peas.

40 Salmon Cheese Casserole

GREAT BRITAIN

SERVES FOUR

1 $\frac{1}{2}$ cups ready-cooked rice
1 can (7 oz.) salmon, drained and flaked
6 oz. shredded cheddar cheese
2 medium tomatoes, peeled and thinly sliced
1 small onion, finely chopped
1 dessertspoon finely-chopped parsley
3 dessertspoons flour
1 $\frac{2}{3}$ cups milk
2 oz. butter
$\frac{1}{4}$ teaspoon ground mace
pinch of cayenne pepper
1 teaspoon salt
salt and pepper
chopped parsley (for garnish)

Melt the butter in a saucepan, add the flour and salt then let cook for a few minutes. Stir in the milk gradually and bring to the boil. Add the shredded cheese and continue cooking, stirring constantly until the sauce is smooth. Season with salt and pepper. Combine the cooked rice with the parsley, cayenne pepper and mace. Spoon into a casserole and cover with most of the tomato. Top with the onion and salmon. Pour over the cheese sauce and garnish with the remainder of the tomato. Bake in an oven at moderate temperature for 15 minutes until heated through. Garnish with the chopped parsley.

41 Beef Carrots

GREAT BRITAIN

SERVES FOUR

4 cups ready-cooked rice
1 lb. rump steak (thickly-cut)
1 lb. carrots
3 onions
3 tablespoons plain flour
$\frac{1}{2}$ cup red wine
$\frac{1}{2}$ pint stock
2 tablespoons oil
pinch of dried herbs
salt and pepper

Cut the steak into 8 strips, then wrap each strip around a long piece of carrot and secure with thread. Cut the onions and the remainder of the carrots into rings, fry until brown in the heated oil, then transfer to a casserole-dish. Fry the Beef Carrots until brown and place them on top of the vegetables. Add the flour to the oil and stir until brown, pour in the stock and stir until boiling. Season well and pour the gravy and wine into the casserole, then add the herbs, salt and pepper. Cover with a lid and cook gently for 1$\frac{1}{2}$–2 hours.

Place the hot rice onto a serving-dish and spoon the Beef Carrots and vegetables and gravy over.

42 Baked Stuffed Fish

GREAT BRITAIN

SERVES FOUR TO SIX

1 $\frac{1}{2}$ cups ready-cooked rice
1 whole fish (4–5 lb.)
1 teaspoon finely-chopped onion
1 oz. melted butter
1 teaspoon mixed herbs
$\frac{1}{2}$ teaspoon salt
freshly-ground pepper

Prepare the fish, and split open. Mix together all the other ingredients and stuff the fish with the mixture. Sew up or skewer the opening. Place on a well-greased baking-dish, cover with buttered foil, and bake in an oven at a moderate temperature for 45–50 minutes. Remove the foil just before the dish is cooked (to brown).

Serve with lemon-butter sauce.

Salmon Cheese Casserole

43 Old English Rice Pudding

GREAT BRITAIN

2 tablespoons uncooked rice
1 tablespoon sugar
2 cups milk
1 teaspoon butter
1 bay leaf
½ teaspoon salt

Place the milk and rice in an oven-proof casserole or pie-dish. Into the rice and milk, stir the sugar and salt, add the bay leaf and stir again. Finally add the butter. Put the pudding into the oven (300°) and bake for ½ hour. Take out the dish, stir the rice with a fork, then bake for another ½ hour. Take out the dish again, stir in a similar manner, then reduce the heat to 250° and bake for 1 hour longer without disturbing it (2 hours baking-time altogether). If using an electric oven, turn the heat off completely for the last ½ hour.

This dish can be served on its own, or with jam or syrup.

44 Brown Rice and Treacle Pudding

GREAT BRITAIN

SERVES FOUR
4 tablespoons uncooked brown rice
whipped cream
1 pint milk
1 tablespoon golden syrup
butter
bay leaf

In an oven-proof dish, blend together the rice and golden syrup. Gradually add the milk. Dot with the butter and lay a bay leaf on top. Bake in a slow oven for approximately 1½ hours, adding more milk if necessary.

Serve hot or cold, with whipped cream pulled into peaks.

45 Pears with Creamy Rice

GREAT BRITAIN

3 cups Creamy Rice
(see recipe page 2)
1 tin pear halves, drained
(reserve syrup)
⅓ cup brown sugar
1 oz. slivered almonds
grated rind of 1 lemon

Place the rice in an oven-proof dish and arrange the pear halves on top. Heat the pear syrup until the liquid has been reduced by half and is slightly thick. Pour the syrup over the pears. Sprinkle with brown sugar, lemon rind and slivered almonds and bake in an oven at moderate temperature for 20–25 minutes.

46 Loganberry Applebake

SERVES SIX

$\frac{1}{2}$ cup uncooked rice
6 cooking apples
3 tablespoons sugar
6 tablespoons loganberry conserve
$3\frac{1}{2}$ cups milk
1 oz. butter
2 teaspoons grated lemon rind
pinch of salt

Bring the milk, lemon rind and salt to the boil. Add the rice and simmer uncovered until tender and most of the milk has been absorbed. Stir in the butter and sugar. Peel and core the apples and place them in a large casserole. Fill each apple with a tablespoonful of loganberry conserve. Carefully spoon the hot rice mixture around the apples. Cover and bake in an oven at moderate temperature for $\frac{3}{4}$ hour until just tender. Cooking time will depend on the variety of apples used.

Serve hot with whipped cream.

47 Fiesta Rice Dessert

GREAT BRITAIN

SERVES SIX

1 ⅔ cups uncooked rice
4 large cooking apples (plus sugar to taste)
¾ cup sugar
1 tablespoon rum
4 cups milk
3 tablespoons hot water
1 tablespoon butter
juice of 1 orange
juice of 1 lemon
½ teaspoon salt
Meringue

Stew the apples and set them aside to cool. Add the uncooked rice to the boiling milk with the salt, and simmer until the rice is tender (approximately 30 minutes). Brown the butter and sugar in a separate saucepan, add the hot water and fruit juices and bring them to the boil. Pour this mixture into the cooked milk rice and simmer for 3 minutes, stirring constantly. Remove the saucepan from the heat, allow to cool a little and then add the rum.

Set the mixture aside until it is cool, then spread a layer of the rice mixture in an oven-proof dish and cover with a layer of cooked apples. Fill the dish alternately with layers of rice and apples until all the ingredients are used. Spread the top with the stiffly-beaten Meringue in a lattice pattern, or completely cover the top. Bake in a slow oven until the Meringue is set but not too brown (approximately 10 minutes). Decorate with chocolate fingers or cherries as desired.

Serve hot or cold, with custard made from the remaining egg-yolks.

Meringue

2 egg-whites
2 tablespoons sugar

Beat the egg-whites until stiff, then gradually add the sugar.

48 Peachy Rice of the Ritz

GREAT BRITAIN

⅔ cup uncooked rice
2 eggs, separated
1 large tin sliced peaches
1 dessertspoon cornflour
4 oz. sugar
1¼ pints milk
1 teaspoon vanilla essence

Drain the peaches and reserve ½ pint of the syrup for a sauce. Add the remaining syrup to the milk. Cook the rice in the milk with 3 oz. of the sugar until most of the liquid has been absorbed. Remove from the heat and stir the egg-yolks and vanilla through the rice, then pour into an oven-proof dish. Beat the egg-whites until stiff, gradually adding 1 oz. sugar. Pipe or spoon the meringue around the edges of the dish, and bake in a slow oven for 40–45 minutes, until the meringue is set and golden. Thicken the peach syrup with the cornflour and cook until thick and clear. Pile sliced peaches in the centre of the dish and cover with the hot sauce.

49 Rosy Apple Rice Dessert

GREAT BRITAIN

SERVES EIGHT
4 cups ready-cooked rice
1 egg, beaten
2 cooking apples
1 cup light brown sugar
½ cup walnut pieces
½ cup honey
⅔ cup milk
½ cup butter
1 teaspoon mixed spice
red food colouring

Melt the butter in a saucepan. Cut each unpeeled apple into 4–5 slices and remove the core. Add the honey and apples to the butter, then mix in the red food colouring until the apples are tinted red. Arrange the apples in the bottom of a deep oven-ware dish (or a round 7″ cake-tin) then place the walnut pieces into the spaces. To the hot rice add the spice, milk, brown sugar and the egg. Carefully spoon over the apple-nut mixture so as not to disturb it. Bake in an oven at a moderate temperature for approximately 50 minutes, until the rice pulls away from the sides of the dish and most of the butter has been absorbed.

Remove from the oven and allow to stand for 10–15 minutes. Turn the dessert out onto the serving-plate.

Serve warm, with whipped cream or vanilla ice-cream.

50 Rice Custard Castle

GREAT BRITAIN

½ cup ready-cooked rice
2 tablespoons custard powder
2 tablespoons sugar
1 pint milk
2 drops vanilla

Place tinned or fresh fruit in the bottom of 4 individual moulds (or 1 large mould). Blend the custard powder with 2 tablespoons milk, place the remaining milk and sugar in a saucepan and heat. Just before boiling, add the cooked rice and the vanilla. Bring to the boil, then quickly remove from the heat and stir in the blended custard powder. Return to the heat and cook for 2 minutes longer. Pour into moulds and stand in a cool place to set. Turn out onto plates, and garnish with more fruit.

Peachy Ric
the R

51 Rhubarb Surprise Pie

GREAT BRITAIN

SERVES SIX

1 cup ready-cooked rice
4 cups sliced rhubarb
¾ cup plain flour
1 teaspoon cornflour
1½ cups sugar
1 teaspoon baking powder
½ cup milk
½ cup boiling water
¼ cup butter
pinch of salt

Wash the rhubarb and cut it into ½" pieces. Arrange them into a greased oven-ware dish. Sift the flour, salt and baking powder together and add the rice. Melt the butter and blend it into ¾ cup of the sugar, then stir into the other dry ingredients alternately with the milk. Spread over the rhubarb. Combine the remaining ¾ cup sugar with the cornflour and sprinkle it over the batter. Pour the boiling water over all and bake in an oven at moderate temperature for 1 hour.

Serve warm, with custard or cream.

52 Rice Biscuits

GREAT BRITAIN

4 oz. ground rice
1 egg
3¾ oz. plain flour
½ teaspoon baking powder
4 oz. castor sugar
blanched almonds
3 oz. butter
1 teaspoon lemon juice
½ teaspoon vanilla
¼ teaspoon salt

Put the sugar and butter in a warm bowl, cream together until smooth and add the vanilla and lemon juice. Sift the dry ingredients thoroughly. Blend in 2 teaspoons of the flour/ground rice mixture to the creamed mixture, then add 1 egg and beat it well in. Add the remainder of the dry ingredients and mix (the dough will be sticky). With well-floured hands, form the mixture into small balls and place on ungreased baking-trays. Flatten into rounds with a fork and stick a blanched almond half on each one. Bake in an oven (350°) for approximately 15–20 minutes, until a golden colour.

53 Strawberry Rice Custard Parfait

GREAT BRITAIN

SERVES SIX

2 cups ready-cooked rice
1 punnet strawberries, sliced cross-wise
¾ cup desiccated coconut
3 tablespoons custard powder (blended with a little milk)
2 tablespoons sugar
½ pint whipped cream
1 pint milk

Place the rice in a basin and set aside. Meanwhile, heat the milk and add the blended custard powder and sugar. Stir over the heat until thickened and smooth, then pour into the basin with the rice. Mix well together and place in the refrigerator to cool. When the rice custard is cool, fold in half the whipped cream.

Place a small quantity of sliced strawberries into 6 parfait glasses, or over the base of a glass dessert bowl. Sprinkle with coconut, then add 2 tablespoons rice custard (more if using a dessert bowl). Repeat this process until the parfait glass or bowl is full. Finish with a layer of rice custard, then add a little of the remaining cream to each, and top with a strawberry slice. These parfaits may be served at once, or chilled.

Strawberry
Custard Par

54 Choco-Rum Baked Rice

GREAT BRITAIN

½ cup uncooked rice
2 eggs
2 tablespoons sugar
4 oz. grated chocolate
2 tablespoons rum
4 cups milk
1 oz. butter

Beat the eggs thoroughly and place in a greased oven-proof dish with the rice, milk and sugar. Stir in 1 tablespoon rum and 3 oz. grated chocolate. Bake in an oven at moderate temperature. Sprinkle with the remainder of the grated chocolate.

Serve hot, with a chocolate sauce, to which has been added the other tablespoon of rum.

55 Apricot Rice Meringue

GREAT BRITAIN

SERVES SIX
2 cups ready-cooked rice
2 eggs
1 can (16 oz.) apricot halves
½ cup apricot syrup (reserved from the can)
2 tablespoons castor sugar
½ can sweetened condensed milk
½ teaspoon vanilla

Combine the rice, condensed milk, syrup and vanilla in a saucepan. Stir until boiling and simmer for 2–3 minutes. Cool slightly and beat in the egg-yolks. Turn into a buttered oven-proof dish, then top with apricots. Beat the egg-whites until very stiff and continue beating, gradually adding the sugar. Pile this meringue on top of the apricots, pulling into peaks. Place in an oven at moderate temperature (325°–350°) for 20 minutes, and serve immediately. *(Illustration page 49)*.

56 Baked Rice Pudding

GREAT BRITAIN

SERVES FIVE TO SIX
3 cups ready-cooked rice
4 eggs
puff-pastry
¼ lb. sugar
¼ lb. currants or raisins
2 tablespoons brandy
1 pint milk
2 oz. beef marrow
2 oz. butter
rind of ½ lemon
nutmeg

Put the lemon-rind and milk into a saucepan and let it infuse until the milk is well-flavoured with the lemon. Beat the eggs and stir in the milk (which should be strained), the butter, marrow, currants and remaining ingredients. Add the rice and mix all together. Line a dish with puff-pastry, put in the pudding and bake for approximately ¾ hour in a slow oven.

57 Avgolemono (Rice and Lemon Soup)

GREECE

2 oz. uncooked rice
2 eggs
2 pints chicken broth (strained)
juice of 1 lemon

Bring the broth to the boil and cook the rice in it until very tender. Beat the eggs with the lemon. Add a little hot broth to the egg mixture, stirring all the time, then add the egg mixture to the rest of the broth. Stir over a very gentle heat for a few minutes. Do not allow to boil.

Choco-R
Baked

58 Dolmádés

GREECE

2 cups ready-cooked rice
36 vine leaves
chopped fried onion
1 cup tomato juice
olive oil
lemon juice

Blanch the vine leaves in boiling, salted water. On the inside of each leaf lay a teaspoon of the rice, and then fold the leaf up like a parcel and squeeze it in the palm of your hand—in this way, the dolmádés will stay rolled up and need not be tied. When they are all ready, put them carefully into a shallow pan, squeeze over plenty of lemon juice and add the tomato juice (enough to come half-way up the pile of dolmádés). Cover with a small plate resting on top of the dolmádés to prevent their moving during cooking, and keep them just simmering for approximately 30 minutes.

Serve them cold. They are a good cocktail snack.

If vine leaves are not available, other leaves (such as cabbage leaves) may be used. In southern Italy a similar dish is made using fig leaves.

59 Dolmas (Stuffed Cabbage)

GREECE

½ cup uncooked rice
1 lb. minced lean meat (beef, lamb, or veal)
1 large cabbage
2 onions, chopped
½ cup sultanas
1 cup yoghurt
butter
½ teaspoon salt
pepper
Sauce

Soak the sultanas in ½ cup boiling water. Bring a large pan of water to the boil and put in the cabbage. Cook the cabbage for 5–10 minutes, just until the leaves are soft and can be separated. Remove the cabbage and drain. Cool slightly, then carefully peel off the leaves, cutting them off the hard centre core. Allow two leaves for each person if you are making this as a main dish.

Sauté the onions in butter for 5 minutes, then mix them with the rice and meat. Add the salt and pepper and the drained sultanas. Take a cabbage leaf, put a heaped spoon of the meat mixture in the centre, and roll up the leaf. Make the roll loose because the rice will swell in cooking. Wrap a piece of thread round each roll and lay carefully in a large dish. Pour one cup of warm water over them, cover the dish, and leave to simmer (or bake in a slow oven) for ½ hour until the rice is tender (test with a fine skewer). Finish off by baking for 10 minutes in a hot oven. Remove the thread, and serve with the Sauce and yoghurt.

Sauce

2 tablespoons thick cream
½ can tomato paste
squeeze of lemon

Dilute the tomato paste with a little water, add the lemon juice, and heat but do not boil. At the last minute, stir in the cream.

Apricot Rice Meri
(Recipe No.

60 Brown Rice Pilaff

GREECE

½ cup uncooked brown rice
1 cup sliced mushrooms
½ cup thinly-sliced celery
½ cup chopped onion
1 ¼ cups boiling chicken stock
pinch of dried thyme
1 teaspoon salt
¼ teaspoon white pepper

To a 1-quart casserole, add the stock then all the remaining ingredients (except the celery). Bake, covered, in an oven at 350° for 70 minutes. Stir in the celery with a fork, then bake for a further 10 minutes. Just before serving, fluff up the rice with a fork.

Golden Rice Salad (opposite)

61 Golden Rice Salad

GREECE

SERVES EIGHT

4½ cups ready-cooked rice
3 hard-boiled eggs, diced
1½ cups sliced celery
1 small onion, minced
1 cup ripe olives, cut into large pieces
¼ cup pimiento
2 tablespoons vinegar
½ cup mayonnaise
¼ cup olive oil
2 tablespoons prepared mustard
1½ teaspoons salt
⅛ teaspoon pepper

Blend together the olive oil, vinegar, mustard, salt and pepper. Pour this mixture over the hot rice, toss, and set aside to cool. Add the remaining ingredients, toss, and chill thoroughly.

Serve on lettuce leaves, and garnish with extra sliced eggs.

62 Chicken Pilaff

GREECE

SERVES FOUR TO SIX

2 cups uncooked medium-grain rice
2 cups cooked chicken, cut into strips
2 medium tomatoes, peeled, seeded and chopped
1 tablespoon finely-chopped onion
⅓ cup coarsely-chopped walnuts
4 cups boiling chicken stock
4 oz. butter
¼ teaspoon ground coriander
1 teaspoon salt
½ teaspoon pepper

Melt the butter in a saucepan, add the chicken and heat gently for 3 minutes. Add the walnuts, cook for 2 minutes longer, then add the onion, salt, pepper, coriander and the rice, and cook for 5 minutes, stirring all the time. Pour on the boiling stock, add the tomatoes and bring to the boil. Cover and simmer for 10 minutes, until the rice is tender and the liquid is completely absorbed. Remove from the heat and allow to stand for 5 minutes before serving.

Serve with a mixed green salad.

63 Rice à la Grecque

GREECE

1 cup uncooked medium-grain rice
2 fresh pork sausages, sliced
3 mushrooms, sliced
½ cup cooked peas
3–4 lettuce leaves, shredded
3 tomatoes, peeled, seeded and diced
1 onion, chopped
1 pimiento, diced
1 small clove garlic, crushed
2 tablespoons raisins (sautéed in butter)
2 cups chicken broth
3 oz. unsalted butter
1 teaspoon salt
dash of freshly-ground black pepper

Melt 2 oz. of the butter in a large saucepan and brown the onion in it. Add the garlic, the sausages, mushrooms and tomatoes, then add the rice and mix well together. Add the chicken broth, salt and pepper. Cover tightly and cook over a low heat for 20 minutes. Mix well with a fork and add the remaining ingredients. May be served alone or with poultry.

This recipe is also suitable for stuffing poultry or veal. In this case, cook for only 15 minutes.

64 Pilaff à la Grecque

GREECE

1 cup uncooked medium-grain rice
½ lb. prawns
1 large onion, chopped
¾ cup chopped green-red peppers
1 tablespoon tomato paste
3 cups water
3 tablespoons olive oil
1 tablespoon lemon juice
1 ½ teaspoons salt
½ teaspoon pepper

Heat the oil in a saucepan and sauté the onions until they are lightly browned. Now stir in the rice and cook until it becomes lightly tinted brown. Add the salt, pepper, tomato paste, chopped peppers and water and simmer slowly for 15 minutes, with the lid on. Then add the lemon juice and prawns, cover and simmer for a further 5–10 minutes, until the rice is cooked and most of the liquid is absorbed.

65 Stuffed Tomatoes à la Grecque

GREECE

2 cups ready-cooked rice
lamb or beef
12 large tomatoes
2 tablespoons chopped onion
chopped garlic
2 tablespoons currants
olive oil
salt and pepper

Cut off the tops of the tomatoes, scoop out the flesh and mix it with the rice. To this mixture add the onion, currants, garlic, pepper, salt and meat (cut into very small pieces). Stuff the tomatoes with this mixture and bake them in a covered dish in the oven with olive oil.

Capsicums may be used instead of tomatoes.

52 *Stuffed Tomatoes à la Grecque*

Pilaff à la Grecque

66 Capsicum Cornucopia

GREECE

SERVES 4
6 oz. uncooked rice
3 oz. mushrooms, chopped
1 medium onion, finely chopped
1 clove garlic, crushed
6 red or green capsicums (of even size)
1 dessertspoon finely-chopped parsley
¾ pint meat or vegetable stock
3 tablespoons tomato purée
1 oz. butter
¼ teaspoon chilli powder
salt and pepper

Blanch the capsicums for 5 minutes in salted water, drain, cut off the tops and scoop out the seeds. Soften the onion with garlic and chilli powder in butter, then add the chopped mushrooms. Sauté this mixture lightly in a pan, then add the rice and sauté for a few minutes longer. Add the parsley, stock, tomato purée and seasonings and bring to the boil. Cover and cook at a moderate temperature for 20–25 minutes, until the rice is tender and all the liquid is absorbed.

Fill the capsicums well with the rice and replace the tops. Brush with melted butter and arrange in an oven-proof dish. Cook in an oven at a moderate temperature for 30 minutes.

67 Continental Rice Cake

GREECE

8 oz. ready-cooked rice
3 eggs
1 tablespoon cornflour
2 oz. castor sugar
½ cup breadcrumbs
½ cup (4 oz.) condensed milk
¼ oz. butter (for cake-tin)
grated rind of 1 lemon

Separate the eggs and beat the whites until very stiff. Continue beating, gradually adding the sugar. Fold in the condensed milk, beaten yolks, rice, cornflour and lemon rind. Toss the breadcrumbs in a well-buttered 7″ cake-tin, then turn the mixture into it. Place in an oven heated to 425°, immediately turn the thermostat to 300° and cook for 30–35 minutes, until set. Loosen the edges with a knife and turn onto a cake cooler.

Top with cherries or other fruit, cinnamon, jam, dessert sauces, etc.

Serve either hot or cold. *(Illustration page 56).*

68 Dutch Oven Meat Balls with Chervil Rice

HOLLAND

½ cup ready-cooked rice
1 cup uncooked rice
1½ lb. minced steak
1 egg, beaten
1 cup green peas
1 onion, sliced
1 cup red wine
½ cup sour cream
1½ cups stock
2 teaspoons chopped chervil
pinch of thyme
salt and pepper

Thoroughly mix the minced steak, cooked rice, egg, salt, pepper and thyme together, then shape into balls approximately 1″ in diameter. Arrange the meat balls in the base of a deep casserole and cover with the onion slices, stock, wine and chervil. Season with salt and pepper. Cover and cook in an oven at a moderate temperature for 1–1¼ hours.

Cook the uncooked rice in boiling, salted water for 10 minutes. Drain, and combine with the peas and sour cream, and fold lightly into the casserole. Return to the moderate-temperature oven and cook for a further 35–40 minutes.

 Continental Rice Cake (Recipe No. 67)

69 Dutch Rice Curry Casserole

HOLLAND

SERVES FOUR TO SIX

2 cups uncooked brown rice
2 lb. blade steak, diced
1 small can pineapple pieces (and syrup)
1 cup sliced celery (large pieces)
2 large carrots, cut into large pieces
2 large onions, cut into large pieces
1 clove garlic, crushed
½ cup desiccated coconut
2 cups beef stock
2 tablespoons oil
3 tablespoons curry powder
salt and pepper

Heat the oil in a casserole-dish and sauté the curry powder with the clove of garlic. Add the meat and brown thoroughly on all sides. Add the vegetables to the casserole and sauté them, by which time the oil should have been absorbed. Now add the pineapple and juice, the stock, pepper, salt and rice, stir lightly to combine everything and cover with a good-fitting lid. Bake in an oven at moderate temperature for 2½–3 hours. Sprinkle with the coconut, and serve very hot.

70 Dutch Curry and Rice Soup

HOLLAND

1 ½ cups ready-cooked rice
2 apples, diced
2 onions, chopped
1 oz. flour
4 pints stock
1 ½ tablespoons butter
1 tablespoon lemon juice
2 teaspoons curry powder

Sauté the onions in butter until golden. Stir in the flour, curry powder, apples and stock. Stir until boiling, then simmer for 1 hour. Rub through a sieve or strainer, then return the soup to the saucepan. Add the lemon juice and cooked rice. Season to taste with salt and pepper. Re-heat the soup, and serve.

71 Stuffed Edam Cheese

HOLLAND

SERVES EIGHT
1 ½ cups ready-cooked rice
1 ½ cups boiled, boned fish
1 Edam cheese (3 lb.)
2 eggs
2 tomatoes, peeled and chopped
1 onion, minced
10 stuffed olives, chopped
¼ cup raisins or currants
2 tablespoons sour pickles, chopped
salt and pepper

Carefully cut the top from the Edam cheese. Scoop out the cheese, leaving ½" shell. Cover with cold water and soak for 1 hour then remove the red rind by gently scraping with a small knife.

Mix together the fish, onion and tomatoes and season to taste with salt and pepper. Cook in melted butter until lightly-browned. Beat the eggs in a bowl until foamy. Grate the cheese (scooped out of the shell) and add, with the rice, raisins or currants, pickles and olives and mix well. Combine the fish and rice mixtures.

Fill the hollowed cheese shell with the mixture and replace the top. Place in a greased 2-quart baking-dish deep enough to hold the stuffed Edam cheese. Bake in an oven at moderate temperature (350°) for approximately 1½ hours.

72 Czardaz Veal with Caraway Rice

HUNGARY

Caraway Rice
3 lb. boned breast of veal
1 cup pineapple pieces
½ cup chopped celery
1 onion, sliced
1 tablespoon chopped parsley
1 tablespoon sugar
1 cup tomato purée
¼ cup barbecue sauce
1 dessertspoon Worcestershire Sauce
2 tablespoons oil

Cut the veal into 2" cubes, then brown the meat on all sides in oil. Add the remaining ingredients to the meat, and mix thoroughly. Season with salt and pepper. Cover and simmer gently for 1½–2 hours, until tender. Remove the cover during the last 15 minutes of cooking time. Add the pineapple pieces and serve.

Serve the Veal over the Caraway Rice.
(Illustration page 61).

Caraway Rice

1 ½ cups uncooked rice
1 ½ teaspoons caraway seeds

Cook the rice in boiling, salted water for 12–15 minutes. Drain, then gently toss the caraway seeds through the rice.

Dutch Curry and Rice

73 Erdélyi Rakott Káposzta (Transylvanian Layered Cabbage) HUNGARY

SERVES EIGHT
3 cups ready-cooked rice
2 lb. boneless pork, cut into $^3/_4$'' cubes
1 lb. Polish or Italian sausage, cut into $^1/_8$'' slices
1 lb. solid piece of bacon, with rind
2 lb. sauerkraut
1 $^1/_2$ cups finely-chopped onions
1 teaspoon finely-chopped garlic
1 $^1/_2$ cups sour cream
$^3/_4$ cup milk
2 cups chicken stock
2 tablespoons paprika
salt
freshly-ground black pepper

Soak the sauerkraut in cold water for 10–20 minutes (to reduce its sourness) then squeeze it dry. Remove the bacon rind and dice the bacon into $^1/_4$'' cubes. In a heavy saucepan, cook the bacon until it is slightly crisp then transfer it to a large mixing-bowl.

Sprinkle the pork cubes with salt and black pepper. Heat 2 tablespoons of the bacon fat in the saucepan then add the pork cubes. Over a medium heat, toss them about for 5–6 minutes until they are lightly browned on all sides. Transfer the pork to the mixing-bowl with the bacon and add the onions and garlic to the fat remaining in the saucepan. Stirring occasionally, cook them for 5 minutes until the onions are lightly coloured. Stir in 2 tablespoons of paprika then add the mixture to the bacon and pork in the mixing-bowl.

Return the saucepan to the heat, add the sausage and cook until it is lightly browned (using more bacon fat if necessary). Transfer the sausage to the mixing-bowl. Add 1 cup of the stock to the saucepan and bring it to the boil, then pour it over all the ingredients in the bowl, mixing thoroughly with the other ingredients.

Line a 6-quart casserole with the sauerkraut (after pulling it apart with your fingers). Spread the meat/onion mixture over the sauerkraut, then spread the rice on top of that. Combine the sour cream and milk and pour the mixture evenly over the rice. Score the bacon rind and cut it into 5–6 equal strips. Distribute these over the top of the casserole and sprinkle with $^1/_2$ teaspoon salt, paprika and pepper. Cook uncovered in the middle of an oven at moderate temperature for 1$^1/_2$ hours, adding the other cup of stock after 1 hour. Serve directly from the casserole.

74 Letsho HUNGARY

1 cup uncooked rice
4 eggs
4 tomatoes, peeled and chopped
1 onion, chopped
2 capsicums, thinly sliced
2 tablespoons lard
1 teaspoon paprika
salt and pepper

Heat the fat in a saucepan and fry the onion until golden-brown. Sprinkle in the rice and paprika and fry for 4 minutes. Add the capsicums, tomatoes, $^1/_2$ cup water, salt and pepper. Cover and cook for 10 minutes. Beat the eggs, pour them into the saucepan and stir the mixture until the eggs are set.

Serve at once.

Czardaz Veal with Caraway Rice
(Recipe No. 72)

75 Risotto con Uovi

ITALY

½ cup uncooked medium-grain rice
4 eggs, poached
½ cup grated cheese
2 tablespoons plain flour
1 cup tomato juice
1 ½ cups boiling water
2 tablespoons butter
salt and pepper

Cook the rice in the water until tender, drain, and then set aside to keep warm. Heat the butter in a saucepan, blend in the flour, then stir in the tomato juice a little at a time until a thick smooth tomato sauce is formed. Stir in ¼ cup grated cheese. Press the warm rice into a flat-bottomed mould, then turn out onto a serving-plate. Place the poached eggs on top of the rice, top with the sauce, then sprinkle the remaining grated cheese on the top.

76 Risotto alla Marinara

ITALY

2 cups uncooked medium-grain rice
2 cups small prawns, shelled
8 anchovy fillets, finely chopped
grated parmesan cheese
2 medium onions, chopped
2 teaspoons chopped parsley
½ cup dry white wine
2 tablespoons tomato paste
2 cups water
2 tablespoons olive oil
1 teaspoon powdered sage
¼ teaspoon salt
pinch of pepper

Heat the oil and add the onions and sauté until golden. When the onions are soft, add the anchovies and cook for 5 minutes. Add the tomato paste and half the water and simmer covered for 20 minutes. Add the parsley, rice, sage, salt and pepper, then add the wine and cook until the wine is somewhat evaporated. Add the remaining water and cook until the rice is tender (approximately 10 minutes). If the rice becomes too dry whilst cooking, add a little more water. Add the prawns in the last 5 minutes of cooking-time.

Serve sprinkled with the grated parmesan cheese.

Other seafood (lobster or crayfish pieces, calimiri, mussels or scallops) may be added to this dish in the last few minutes of cooking.

77 Braised Chicken with Rice

ITALY

SERVES SIX
4 cups ready-cooked rice
1 boiling fowl
2 eggs
carrot rings
green vegetables
2 onions, sliced
1 clove garlic, crushed
4 tablespoons flour
2 oz. finely-chopped almonds
2 oz. finely-chopped walnuts
½ cup cream
½ cup tomato purée
1 cup stock (or water)
3 tablespoons butter
1 teaspoon dried marjoram
1 teaspoon dried thyme
salt and pepper

Wash and dry the boiling fowl and cut it into serving pieces. Dip the poultry into the flour (which has been mixed with the salt, pepper, marjoram and thyme). Heat the butter in a pan and brown the meat all over. Lift out the meat, add the onion and garlic, and brown. Then return the meat to the pan and add the stock and tomato purée. Cover the pan and simmer gently for 1–1¼ hours. Strain off the stock and keep it hot. Beat the eggs thoroughly then very slowly add ½ pint of the hot stock, beating all the time. Stir in the nuts and cream. Re-heat the sauce, but do not allow it to boil. Place the hot rice onto a platter, the chicken on top, then cover with the sauce.

Serve with a green vegetable and carrot rings.

78 Prawn Calabrese

ITALY

3 cups ready-cooked rice
2 lb. prawns, shelled
½ cup grated carrot
2 tomatoes, peeled and diced
1 cup chopped onion
1 clove garlic, crushed
¼ cup chopped parsley
1 tablespoon flour
2 teaspoons sugar
½ cup beef broth
3 tablespoons water
1 dessertspoon butter
2 dessertspoons lemon juice
⅛ teaspoon saffron
pinch of cayenne
1 teaspoon salt
pinch of pepper

Melt the butter in a large pan, then add the garlic, onion and carrot. Cook over a low heat for 10 minutes, then add the tomatoes, broth, lemon juice, sugar, salt, pepper, cayenne and saffron. Cover and simmer gently for approximately 15 minutes, then add the prawns and parsley and cook for a further 10–15 minutes. Blend the flour and water together and stir into the mixture. Stir until it thickens, then cook for 2 minutes.

Serve in coupe dishes with the rice.

79 Suppli al Telefono (Deep-fried Rice-and-Cheese Balls)

ITALY

SERVES FOUR TO SIX

2 cups ready-cooked rice
2 eggs
4 oz. mozzarella cheese, cut into ½″ cubes
¾ cup fine dry breadcrumbs
vegetable oil (for deep-frying)
parsley (for garnish)

Beat the eggs lightly with a fork until they are just combined. Then add the rice and stir gently but thoroughly, taking care not to mash the rice. Scoop up 1 tablespoon of the mixture in a spoon, place a cube of mozzarella in the middle, and top with another spoonful of rice. Press the two spoons together, or use your hands to shape a ball. Roll the ball in breadcrumbs and place on wax paper. Similarly, shape other balls. The balls may be fried at once, but they are easier to handle if refrigerated for 30 minutes.

Heat the oil in a deep-fat fryer to 375°. Pre-heat the oven to 250°, line a large baking-dish with blotting paper, and put the dish in the oven. Fry the balls, 4 or 5 at a time, for about 5 minutes until they are golden brown and the cheese has melted. Transfer to the baking-dish to drain. Serve hot.

80 Venetian Risotto

ITALY

1 cup uncooked medium-grain rice
6–8 oz. lean lamb, cut into small squares
¼ lb. tomatoes, peeled and chopped
1 onion, chopped
1 clove garlic, crushed
1 glass white wine
bouillon cubes (for meat broth)
butter

Melt the onion and garlic in the butter, then brown the meat. Add the tomatoes, white wine, salt and pepper, then a little of the stock. Cover the pan and simmer until the meat is nearly cooked. Stir in the rice. Allow the rice to soak up a good deal of the liquid from the meat before adding the remaining meat stock, a little at a time, and finish cooking, adding grated cheese when the rice is almost ready.

81 Chicken Liver Risotto

ITALY

1 cup uncooked medium-grain rice
5 chicken livers, cut into eighths
grated parmesan cheese
½ cup finely-chopped mushroom
½ cup finely-chopped onion
2 tablespoons chopped parsley
2½ cups boiling chicken stock
2 oz. butter

Melt the butter in a heavy saucepan and brown the chicken livers. Remove the livers and keep hot. Add the onion to the saucepan and cook until transparent, then add the chopped mushrooms and cook for 3 minutes longer. Add the rice and cook, stirring constantly, for 2 minutes. Add the stock, cover, and simmer gently over a low heat until the stock is absorbed and the rice is tender but firm (approximately 20 minutes). If the stock is absorbed before the rice is cooked, add a little more liquid. Stir the livers and parsley into the rice, and serve immediately with grated parmesan cheese.

Suppli al Telefono
(Deep-fried Rice-and-Cheese Balls)

82 Risotto con Scampi

ITALY

SERVES SIX TO EIGHT

2 cups uncooked rice
1 lb. medium-size prawns, peeled
2 lb. fish heads and trimmings
½ cup freshly grated parmesan cheese
1 carrot, sliced
2 small onions, sliced
½ teaspoon finely-chopped garlic
2 parsley sprigs
½ cup dry white wine
2 quarts water
9 tablespoons butter
1 bay leaf

In a 3–4 quart saucepan, combine the prawn shells, fish heads and trimmings, water and wine. Bring to the boil over a high heat, removing the scum as it rises to the surface. Add the onions, carrot, parsley and bay leaf, reduce the heat and simmer partially covered for 30 minutes, skimming the stock occasionally. Remove from the heat and strain the stock through a fine sieve into another saucepan, pressing down hard on the trimmings and vegetables with the back of a spoon to extract their juices before discarding them. Set the pan of strained stock over a low heat and let it barely simmer.

In a heavy 8–10″ pan, melt 1 tablespoon butter over a moderate heat. Toss in the prawns and garlic and cook, stirring frequently, for 2–3 minutes. Cover, and set them aside.

Melt 4 tablespoons butter over a moderate heat in a heavy casserole. Add the rice and cook, stirring constantly, for 2–3 minutes until the grains become somewhat opaque. Add 2 cups of simmering stock and cook the rice uncovered over a moderate heat, stirring occasionally, until almost all the liquid is absorbed. Add another 2 cups of stock and cook, stirring again, until it is absorbed. Then add 2 more cups of stock. When this is absorbed, the rice should be tender. If the rice is still too firm, add more stock—½ cup at a time—and continue cooking and stirring until the rice is tender.

With a fork, gently stir in the prawns and garlic and the juice that will have accumulated in the pan. Then stir in 4 tablespoons of soft butter and, finally, the freshly grated parmesan cheese.

Serve the Risotto con Scampi at once, while it is creamy and hot.

83 Risotto à la Norton

ITALY

1 cup uncooked medium-grain rice
4 oz. mushrooms, sliced and cooked gently in butter
2 small white onions, finely chopped
3 cups chicken stock
4 oz. butter
¼ teaspoon saffron
salt
freshly-ground black pepper

Melt the butter in a large frying-pan, add the onions and cook them until they are transparent. Add the rice and a small amount of the chicken stock. Cook, stirring constantly, until the rice is tender, adding stock as it is absorbed. Add the saffron, salt and pepper and serve immediately, garnished with the mushroom slices.

84 Rice and Bacon Salad Bowl

ITALY

SERVES FOUR TO SIX

3 cups ready-cooked rice
½ lb. bacon
1 cup diced cucumber
1 cup diced celery
1 red capsicum, chopped
1 green capsicum, sliced
salt and pepper
French Dressing

Combine the rice, bacon pieces, cucumber, red capsicum and celery in a large bowl, pour on the French Dressing and toss gently until thoroughly blended. Finally add the pieces of sliced green capsicum and chill before serving.

For a special occasion, scoop out the centre of a red or green cabbage and use it as a serving-bowl.

French Dressing

1 clove garlic, crushed
⅔ cup oil
⅓ cup white vinegar
salt and pepper

Place the ingredients into a screw-topped container and shake vigorously, then allow to stand. Shake again before using and remove the garlic.

85 Risotto Milanese

ITALY

SERVES THREE TO FOUR

1 cup uncooked medium-grain rice
shell-fish, mushrooms or chicken
1 oz. grated parmesan cheese
1 onion, finely chopped
1 gill white wine
2 cups well-flavoured stock
3 oz. butter
saffron
salt and pepper

Soak a generous pinch of saffron in a few tablespoons of the hot stock. In a heavy pan, heat 2 oz. butter and let the onion soften. When it turns golden add the rice, turning it over and over in the butter until every grain is transparent and shiny. Add the wine and let it bubble until almost evaporated, before adding ⅔ cup boiling stock. Keep the rest of the stock simmering on the stove until needed. Allow the rice to simmer steadily, stirring occasionally, until most of the liquid has been absorbed before adding any more. The total cooking time is approximately 25 minutes.

Add the saffron near the end of the cooking and, at this stage, stir constantly. When the rice is cooked, season with salt and pepper and stir in the remaining butter and grated cheese.

86 Risi e Bisi

ITALY

2 cups uncooked rice
¼ lb. smoked ham, diced
2 tablespoons grated parmesan cheese
1½ lb. peas
2 spring onions, finely chopped
2 tablespoons finely-chopped parsley
2½–3 pints hot meat stock
2 oz. butter
2 tablespoons olive oil
extra parmesan cheese for garnish

Heat the oil and half the butter in a heavy pan, add the onions and parsley and cook gently. Add the peas and the diced ham and allow to cook long enough to absorb the fat, then add enough hot meat stock to cover and allow to bubble before adding the rice. After adding the rice, add a further ¾ pint heated stock and cook gently, without stirring, for 25–30 minutes, until the rice is cooked. Stir in the remainder of the butter and the 2 tablespoons parmesan cheese.

Serve with the extra parmesan cheese sprinkled over as a garnish.

Rice and I
Salad

87 **Riso al Limone** (Boiled Rice with Lemon)

ITALY

SERVES FOUR

1 cup uncooked rice
3 eggs
1 cup freshly grated parmesan cheese
4 teaspoons lemon juice
6 quarts water
2 tablespoons butter
3 tablespoons salt

In a large saucepan, bring the water and salt to a bubbling boil over a high heat. Pour in the rice in a slow stream so that the water never stops boiling. Stir once or twice, then reduce the heat to moderate and boil the rice, uncovered and undisturbed, for approximately 15 minutes, until it is tender. Test it by tasting a few grains. As soon as the rice is tender, drain it thoroughly in a large colander.

Over a low heat, melt the butter in a 1-quart flameproof casserole dish and immediately add the hot drained rice. In a bowl, beat the eggs with a fork until they are well combined. Then beat in the cheese and lemon juice. Stir this mixture into the rice and cook over a very low heat, stirring gently with a fork, for 3–4 minutes.

Serve at once, while the rice is still creamy.

88 Genoese Rice

ITALY

SERVES FOUR
1 cup uncooked rice
8 oz. salami, diced
4 oz. grated parmesan cheese
8 oz. mushrooms
1 lb. peas
1 onion, chopped
2 pints meat or chicken broth
1 oz. butter

Cook the onion in the butter until just golden, using a heavy pan. Peel and slice the mushrooms. Heat the stock, put in the mushrooms, salami and peas, and simmer gently over a very low heat. Whilst these are cooking, bring plenty of salted water to a brisk boil, then cook the rice in this for 5 minutes. Strain the rice, add to the stock, and simmer, covered, until nearly all the stock has been absorbed. Stir in 2 dessertspoons of the cheese, turn the whole mixture into a fairly deep oven-proof dish, and top with the remainder of the cheese. Bake in an oven at a moderate temperature for approximately 20 minutes, until the cheese topping has turned into a golden crust.

89 Mediterranean Cheese-Rice Salad

ITALY

SERVES FOUR

3 cups ready-cooked rice
1 cup diced Cheddar cheese
1 cup matured Cheddar cheese slivers
1 cup cottage cheese
6 asparagus spears
1 cup chopped celery
tomato wedges
1 capsicum, diced
1 cup olives
¾ cup french dressing

Lightly toss all the ingredients (except the tomato wedges and some of the diced cheese) together in a bowl until the dressing is thoroughly absorbed. Arrange the tomato wedges in a circle on the rice and fill the centre with the remainder of the diced cheese.

90 Milanese Fillets of Beef

ITALY

1 cup uncooked rice
4 slices fillet of beef (¾–1″ thick)
1 tablespoon brandy
2 oz. butter
1 tablespoon Worcestershire Sauce
½ teaspoon prepared mustard
¼ teaspoon powdered rosemary
pepper and salt

Melt the butter in a frying-pan and add the rosemary. Place the fillets of beef into the butter and cook for 2–3 minutes on each side. Season with salt and pepper, then add the Worcestershire Sauce, mustard and brandy. Cook the fillets for a further 2 minutes. Remove the meat from the pan and keep hot. Reduce the liquid over a high heat for 1 minute. Serve the sauce over the fillets.

Cook the rice in boiling, salted water for 12–15 minutes. Drain, and serve with the fillets.

91 Veal Oregano

ITALY

Rice (See below)
2 lb. veal steak, cut into pieces
4 oz. bacon, diced
4 tomatoes, peeled and chopped
1 onion, sliced
1 clove garlic, crushed
2 oz. flour
½ cup red wine
1 oz. butter
½ teaspoon oregano

Combine the flour and ¼ teaspoon oregano, then season with salt and pepper. Toss the steak lightly in the seasoned flour, to coat. Sauté the meat, bacon, onion slices and garlic in the hot butter for 10 minutes. Add the tomatoes, wine, salt and pepper, and the remaining oregano. Cover and simmer gently for 35–45 minutes, until the meat is tender.

Serve on a bed of the Rice.

Rice

1 cup uncooked medium-grain rice
½ onion, finely chopped
1 pint stock
½ oz. butter
½ bay leaf

Sauté the onion lightly in the butter, add the rice and bay leaf and stir over the heat for 1 minute. Add enough stock to come ½″ above the rice. Add salt and pepper, bring to the boil, cover, and simmer very gently until the stock has been absorbed. Remove the bay leaf.

Mediterranean Cheese-Rice Salad

Chicken Italiana with Olive-Cheese Sauce

SERVES SIX

1 ¼ cups uncooked rice
1 chicken(2½-3½ lb.), cut into frying pieces
¾ cup sharp grated cheese
8–12 stuffed olives, chopped
3–4 dessertspoons plain flour
½ cup plain flour
3 cups milk
1 dessertspoon olive juice
lard (for frying chicken)
¼ teaspoon nutmeg
3 teaspoons salt
sprinkle pepper

Place the ½ cup flour, 2 teaspoons salt and the pepper in a paper bag. Add the pieces of raw chicken and shake the bag to coat the chicken with the seasoned flour. Heat ½″ lard in a pan. Brown the chicken briskly on all sides and, when browned, reduce the heat, cover tightly, and cook until tender (approximately 40 minutes), turning as necessary to brown evenly. Uncover for the last 10 minutes, for a crisper crust.

Meanwhile, boil the 1¼ cups of rice, to make 4 cups of drained, salted, boiled rice. Keep this warm until needed to serve. Drain the cooked chicken pieces and then keep hot in a very slow oven.

Pour off the fat in the pan, then measure back 3 tablespoons of this fat into the same pan and place 4 dessertspoons plain flour to one side of the pan. Blend the fat into the flour and cook, stirring, for several minutes. Slowly blend in the milk, then stir in the cheese, nutmeg and 1 teaspoon salt. Cook, stirring, until the Sauce thickens smoothly, then add the chopped olives and olive juice. Add more milk for a thinner Sauce.

Place the rice onto a hot platter. Arrange the chicken pieces over the rice, and top with the delicious Olive-Cheese Sauce.

93 Riso Primavera

ITALY

2 cups uncooked rice
½ lb. ham, thickly sliced
2 oz. grated parmesan cheese
2 oz. butter
White Sauce

Boil the rice in boiling, salted water. When cooked, strain, and blend in the butter and the grated parmesan cheese. Place the rice mixture onto a serving-dish. Prepare the White Sauce. Cut the ham into cubes, add this to the Sauce, then pour this mixture over the rice. Sprinkle grated cheese on top.

White Sauce

2 tablespoons flour
2 cups milk
2 oz. butter

Blend the butter and flour together, then slowly add the milk, stirring constantly, over a very low heat until it is perfectly smooth. Do not allow to boil.

94 Rice Salad Supreme

ITALY

3 cups ready-cooked rice
3-4 anchovy fillets, diced
1 avocado, diced
6 asparagus spears
1 cup diced celery
tomato wedges
1 cup chopped shallots or onions
¼ cup red or green peppers
½ cup stuffed olives
2 tablespoons chopped mint
1 cup mayonnaise
1 dessertspoon capers
salt and pepper

In a large salad bowl, combine all the ingredients. Pour over the mayonnaise. With salad servers toss gently all the ingredients until the mayonnaise is completely blended throughout. Add salt and pepper to taste before serving.

95 Chicken with Tuna Sauce and Rice

ITALY

3 cups ready-cooked rice
1 roasting chicken (3-3½ lb.)
1 can (8 oz.) tuna
1 carrot
1 bunch celery
tomato slices
1 onion, stuck with cloves
sprig of parsley, thyme and marjoram, tied firmly together
1 glass dry white wine
1 cup cream, slightly whipped
½ pint water
½ cup mayonnaise
1 tablespoon french dressing
lemon juice
paprika
salt and pepper

Clean the chicken, wash and dry. Place in a large saucepan with the wine, water, onion, carrot, 1 stick of celery and the herbs. Season with salt and pepper and add the tuna, which should have the oil drained off before adding. Cover the pan and simmer for approximately 1 hour, turning the bird occasionally. Remove from the heat and allow the chicken to cool in the liquid.

Season the french dressing well with paprika, and add to the rice. Arrange the rice on a fairly large serving-dish. Take the chicken out of the liquid, remove the skin, and joint into serving pieces, then arrange these on the rice. Remove the vegetables from the liquid.

Strain the tuna from the liquid, and put into the blender (or beat with a spoon) until smooth. Mix the tuna purée into the mayonnaise, sharpen with the lemon juice, then blend into the cream. Spoon this sauce over the chicken pieces.

Chill this dish well and, just before serving, garnish with tomato slices and celery.

Rice Salad Supreme

96 Italian Green Rice

ITALY

SERVES FOUR
¾ lb. uncooked rice
2 oz. grated parmesan cheese
2 tablespoons cooked spinach, strained
1 clove garlic
¼ lb. butter
½ teaspoon sage

Cook the rice in boiling, salted water for 15–18 minutes. A few minutes before the rice is cooked, gently sauté the garlic and sage in the butter, not allowing the butter to brown. Discard the garlic as soon as it becomes lightly golden. Stir the cooked, strained spinach into the rice and pour the hot butter over it. Mix well. Sprinkle with the grated parmesan cheese, and serve.

97 Osso Buco

ITALY

SERVES SIX
Saffron Rice (see recipe page 3)
2 veal knuckles
1 anchovy fillet, finely chopped
1 medium onion, finely chopped
2 cloves garlic, crushed
2 tablespoons chopped parsley
flour
½ cup dry white wine
1–2 tablespoons tomato paste
½ cup stock
1 tablespoon butter
1 tablespoon olive oil
grated rind of ½ lemon
salt
freshly-ground black pepper

Ask the butcher to saw the knuckles into 2″ pieces. Dredge the pieces with flour, season with salt and pepper, and brown in the olive oil and butter. Add 1 clove garlic and the onion, then pour over the stock, wine and tomato paste. Cover the pan and simmer for 1½ hours. Add the remaining clove garlic and the anchovy fillet. Blend thoroughly, heat through, and serve on a bed of Saffron Rice sprinkled with the chopped parsley and grated lemon rind.

98 Portuguese Risotto with Mushrooms

PORTUGAL

SERVES FOUR

1 ½ cups uncooked medium-grain rice
1 cup diced cooked veal
1 cup finely-grated sharp cheese
¼ lb. mushrooms, finely sliced
1 onion, diced
2 cloves garlic, crushed
1 ½ pints boiling chicken stock
4 tablespoons oil
salt and pepper

Place the oil into a heavy-bottomed frying-pan and heat. Add the onion, garlic and the finely-sliced mushrooms and stalks. As soon as the onion begins to brown, add the rice and stir over the heat until it begins to take on a transparent look. Add the boiling stock, 1 cup at a time, stirring all the time to prevent the rice sticking to the pan. Cook the mixture for 45 minutes, when the rice will have absorbed the liquid. Add the meat, salt and pepper and mix thoroughly until very hot.

Serve at once, with the cheese sprinkled over the top.

99 Russian Salmon

RUSSIA

2 cups ready-cooked rice
1 large can salmon
1 hard-boiled egg
1 pint white sauce
1 tablespoon curry powder
salt and pepper
parsley (for garnish)

Flake the salmon and remove any bones. Add the curry powder to the white sauce. Combine the salmon juice, flaked salmon and boiled rice with the white sauce mixture. Add salt and pepper to taste and mix well together. Place in a greased oven-dish and bake in an oven at a moderate temperature for approximately 15–20 minutes. Cover the dish with foil to prevent the salmon drying out.

Garnish with hard-boiled egg and sprinkle with chopped parsley. *(Illustration page 83).*

100 Danish Rice Pudding

SCANDINAVIA DENMARK

SERVES FOUR

⅓ cup uncooked rice
2 oz. cherries
2 tablespoons sugar
4 oz. sultanas
2 oz. chopped walnuts
2 tablespoons sweet sherry
1 pint milk
1 can evaporated milk
¼ cup cold water
2 tablespoons gelatine
1 tablespoon butter
Chocolate Sauce

Cook the rice in the milk until all the milk has been absorbed. Add the butter and sugar and beat until smooth. Soak the gelatine in the cold water, dissolve over hot water, and then add to the creamed rice. Let this cook and then fold in the whipped evaporated milk, cherries, sultanas, walnuts and sherry. Chill in one large mould or individual moulds.

Serve with the Chocolate Sauce.

Chocolate Sauce

1 ½ tablespoons cornflour
2 tablespoons sugar
2 dessertspoons cocoa
¾ pint milk

Heat the milk and sugar to the boil. Mix the cocoa and cornflour smoothly in a basin with extra milk or water. Add this mixture to the boiling milk, lower the heat and cook for 3 minutes. Serve cold.

Salad Royale with Green Mayonnaise
(Recipe No. 106)

101 Danish Almond Rice

SCANDINAVIA DENMARK

3 cups ready-cooked rice
3 eggs
2 oz. sugar
¼ cup ground almonds
¾ cup sour cream
grated rind of ½ lemon

Beat the eggs with the sugar until the mixture is thick and creamy. Lightly fold the cream, ground almonds, grated lemon rind and rice through the egg mixture. Place in a greased oven-proof dish and bake in an oven at a moderate temperature for 25–30 minutes until lightly browned.

Serve hot or cold.

102 Swedish Rice Porridge

SCANDINAVIA SWEDEN

1 cup uncooked rice
2 dessertspoons sugar
1 blanched almond
1 cup heavy cream
4 cups milk
1 cup raspberry conserve
2 dessertspoons butter
1 teaspoon vanilla extract
1 2″-stick cinnamon
1 teaspoon salt

Melt the butter in a large, heavy saucepan, then add the rice and 1 cup of water. Bring to the boil, and boil uncovered until the water has evaporated (approximately 5–10 minutes). Add the milk and cinnamon stick and simmer uncovered for 35–40 minutes until the rice is tender, stirring occasionally. Remove from the heat and gently stir in the cream, salt, sugar, vanilla, remaining butter and the almond. Melt the raspberry conserve in the top of a double-boiler over boiling water.

Serve the rice porridge hot, with the hot raspberry conserve as a sauce.

This is a recipe which is traditionally served on Christmas Eve in Sweden. The tradition says that whoever gets the almond will marry before the next Christmas.

103 Sasaties

SOUTH AFRICA

SERVES SIXTEEN
ready-cooked white rice
4 lb. fillet of pork, cut into cubes
4 lb. leg of mutton, cut into cubes
4 large onions, sliced
1 tablespoon sugar
2 bay leaves, crumbled
1 tablespoon curry powder
1 tablespoon turmeric
vinegar
paprika
1 teaspoon salt
pepper

Place the meat and onions in a mixing-bowl, seasoning with the salt, pepper and paprika. Add the remainder of the ingredients, using only enough vinegar to cover. If the mixture is too acid, add a little water. The mixture should be slightly sweet. Allow to stand for 24 hours. Remove the meat and put onto skewers, the mutton and pork alternately. Grill over charcoal, if possible. Boil the marinade until the onions are tender, and thicken with corn-starch.

Serve the sauce with the sasaties and bowls of dry white rice.

Danish Almond Rice

Russian Salmon
(Recipe No. 99)

104 Paella à la Catalana

SPAIN

½ lb. uncooked rice
2 oz. fresh pork
2–3 oz. garlic sausage
1 jar mussels (or 12 scallops)
½ lb. fresh peas
2 large tomatoes, sliced
1 onion, sliced
2 peppers, sliced
2 cloves garlic
few almonds and pine nuts
2 oz. pork fat
saffron
parsley

Heat the pork fat in a large casserole, then put in the pork and the sausage (cut into small pieces), together with the sliced onion. Fry for a minute or two, then add the peppers and tomatoes. Simmer for 15 minutes, then add the rice, peas, mussels (or scallops), garlic, almonds, pine nuts and powdered saffron. Pour over 2 pints of boiling water and let the whole mixture bubble for a few minutes, then lower the heat and cook gently until the rice is tender.

Serve in the pan in which it was cooked. Garnish with parsley.

105 Arroz à la Catalana

SPAIN

1 cup uncooked rice
4 oz. pork
2–3 oz. Spanish sausage
1 jar mussels
½ lb. peas
2 large tomatoes, sliced
1 onion, sliced
2 sweet red peppers
2 cloves garlic
few almonds
pinch of saffron
parsley for garnish

Trim the pork and cut it into cubes. Heat the fatty pork in a large casserole, and put in the lean pork and the sausage (which has also been cut into small pieces), together with the sliced onion. Fry for a minute or two, then add the red peppers and sliced tomatoes. Simmer for 15 minutes, then add the rice, peas, mussels, garlic, saffron and almonds. Pour 2 pints of boiling water over the mixture. Allow to boil for a few minutes, then lower the heat and simmer until the rice is tender.

Serve in the pan in which it is cooked. Garnish with parsley.

106 Salad Royale with Green Mayonnaise

SPAIN

SERVES EIGHT

3 cups ready-cooked rice
1 lb. prawns, shelled and deveined
½ lb. lobster
½ lb. crab meat
½ cup chopped celery
1 cup chopped green pepper
1 cup chopped parsley
½ cup French Dressing
1 cup Green Mayonnaise

Place each seafood in separate bowls. Place the chopped celery and green peppers in another bowl. Pour the French Dressing over each, and marinate in the refrigerator for 2 hours.

Pile the rice on a bed of lettuce leaves. Arrange the seafoods and vegetables on top.

Serve with the Green Mayonnaise in a separate bowl.

French Dressing

1 clove garlic
2 tablespoons wine vinegar
6 tablespoons olive oil
salt and pepper

Blend all the ingredients together, and shake well. Refrigerate, then remove the garlic before serving.

Green Mayonnaise

2 tablespoons finely-chopped parsley
1 cup mayonnaise

Combine the parsley and mayonnaise and pour into a serving bowl. *(Illustration page 81).*

Paella à la Cat

107 Suliman's Pilaff

SPAIN

2 cups uncooked rice
mutton, cooked and in small pieces
tomatoes
fried onions
currants
raisins
pine nuts (or roasted almonds)
sour cream (or yoghurt)
4 pints boiling water
3–4 tablespoons oil
garlic

Put the oil into a thick pan. When it is warm, add the rice and stir for a few minutes until the rice takes on a transparent look. Then pour over the boiling water and cook quickly for approximately 12 minutes.

In the meantime, have ready a savoury preparation of small pieces of cooked mutton, fried onions, raisins, currants, garlic, tomatoes and pine nuts (or roasted almonds), all sautéed in oil with plenty of seasoning.

Put the strained rice into a thick pan and stir in the meat and onion mixture, add a little more oil if necessary, and stir for a few minutes over a low heat before serving.

Serve with the Pilaff a bowl of sour cream (or yoghurt).

108 Paella Barcelona

SPAIN

SERVES FOUR TO SIX
8 oz. uncooked rice
2 cups cooked chicken, diced
1 tin clams, drained
1 small can artichoke hearts
1 cup cooked peas
1 onion, chopped
2 red peppers
1 clove garlic
¼ cup blanched almonds, sliced
½ cup tomato purée
3–4 cups chicken stock
3 tablespoons olive oil
pinch of saffron
1 teaspoon paprika
salt and pepper
1 sprig parsley

Heat the olive oil in a paella pan or heavy shallow pan, and sauté the onion and garlic until transparent. Add the rice and cook, stirring, until it begins to colour. Add the tomato purée, chicken stock, chicken (reserve some for garnish), paprika, saffron, half the clams, the peas, salt and pepper and simmer gently for 5 minutes. If the rice should become too dry, add a little more stock.

Garnish with the remainder of the chicken, the clams and the artichokes. Arrange the almonds, red pepper and parsley on top. Serve in the pan, or transfer to a hot serving-platter.

109 Rice Barcelona

SPAIN

1 cup uncooked rice
4 oz. ham
1 cup cooked peas
2 tomatoes, sliced
1 onion, chopped
1 pint stock (or water)
8 oz. butter
pinch grated nutmeg
salt and pepper
chopped parsley

Melt the butter in a large saucepan and fry the onion until golden. Add the ham and sliced tomatoes. Put in the rice, and fry until it changes colour, then add the boiling stock (or water). Boil rapidly for 7 minutes, when the liquid should be almost absorbed. Add the nutmeg and peas, season with salt and pepper, and finish cooking in an oven at moderate temperature for 10–15 minutes.

Paella Barc

11 de agosto
a las 5.30 h.
de SEVILLA

110 Paella

SPAIN

SERVES SIX
3 cups (12 oz.) uncooked long or medium-grain rice
few chicken livers
1 cup cooked lobster
jar or cup mussels
1 cup any other shell-fish (e.g. prawns, oysters)
3 tomatoes
½ cup sliced onions
2 red or green peppers
4 cloves garlic
12 black olives
olive oil
powdered saffron or turmeric

Strain the liquid off the mussels. Fry the sliced onions, peppers, garlic, tomatoes, stoned olives and chicken livers in oil, then add the lobster, prawns, etc., and keep warm. In a large pan, heat 1 cup olive oil, put in the rice and stir until the oil is absorbed. Pour over 2 pints of boiling water, add salt and a good pinch of saffron or turmeric. Cook fairly fast, stirring occasionally, for 12 minutes. Add the liquid from the mussels and cook for approximately 4 minutes. It should by now be tender and have absorbed all the liquid. Add the shell-fish and tomato mixture, then the mussels, and serve quickly, preferably in the pan in which it has been cooked.

111 Paella (Alternative Recipe)

SPAIN

SERVES SIX
3 cups uncooked medium-grain rice
1 spring chicken
8 oz. prawns (leave 12 unpeeled)
1 quart mussels
½ cup cooked peas
1 lb. brown onions, chopped
4 capsicums, chopped (2 red, 2 green)
2 cloves garlic, very thinly sliced
5 cups stock
¼ pint olive oil
seasoned flour
½ teaspoon powdered saffron
paprika

Cut the raw chicken into small pieces, dust with a mixture of the seasoned flour and paprika, then fry in the oil in a large heavy-bottomed pan or paella dish. Remove the chicken and, in the same pan, fry the onions, capsicums, garlic and peeled prawns until lightly browned. Mix in the rice, saffron and peas, then the stock and chicken pieces. Put the pan in an oven at a moderate temperature for 20 minutes, until the rice is cooked and has absorbed the stock. Steam the mussels in white wine until cooked, then add to the mixture.

Garnish the dish with the unpeeled prawns hooked over the rim.

112 Arroz con Pollo

SPAIN

1 lb. uncooked rice
2 chickens (2½ lb. each), cut into serving pieces
½ cup green peas
6 medium tomatoes, peeled and sliced
2 medium onions, thinly sliced
6 shallots, chopped
2 tablespoons chopped parsley
flour (for dredging)
2–3 tablespoons oil
1 large bay leaf
¼ teaspoon saffron (soaked in 2 cups chicken stock)
salt
freshly-ground pepper

Heat the oil, sauté the shallots and onions, then remove them from the pan. In the same oil, gently sauté the chicken pieces, which have been dredged in flour and lightly seasoned with salt and pepper. Brown each piece delicately, turning often to prevent burning. Return the shallots and onion to the pan with the chicken and add the tomatoes, stock, bay leaf and parsley. Cover and simmer until the chicken is almost cooked. Transfer the chicken to a large saucepan, add the rice, and simmer for approximately 15–20 minutes, until the rice is tender.

Asparagus spears and artichoke hearts lightly cooked in butter make a good garnish for this dish. Strips of pimiento make a bright decoration.

113 Arroz con Pollo (Alternative Recipe)

SPAIN

SERVES EIGHT
2 cups uncooked rice
2 chickens (each 4 lb.)
1 cup chopped onions
pimiento strips
green olives, whole
2 cloves garlic, minced
1 cup olive oil
saffron
paprika
salt and pepper
chopped parsley

Use the necks, backs and gizzards of the chickens for a broth. Cut the remainder of the chickens into serving pieces and place in a large saucepan. Season and brown lightly in the olive oil, adding the onions and garlic. Add 5 cups chicken broth. Cover, and cook slowly on top of the stove until the chicken is almost done. Add the rice and 1 teaspoon dissolved saffron. Continue to cook slowly, covered, until the liquid is absorbed and the rice is dry and fluffy. Taste for seasoning without breaking the rice. Add the whole, unpitted green olives.

Serve on a hot platter decorated with the chopped parsley and pimiento strips.

114 Stuffed Pimientos

SPAIN

2 cups ready-cooked rice
pieces of lamb or beef
2 tablespoons chopped onion
12 pimientos
chopped garlic
2 tablespoons currants
tomato purée
olive oil
salt and pepper

Cut the stalks off the pimientos and make a small slit down the side of each one, through which you extract the core and seeds. Wash the pimientos under the tap to be sure of removing all the seeds, which are very fiery.

Stuff the pimientos with a mixture of the rice, onion, currants, garlic, pepper, salt and meat. Put them in a deep baking-dish with a moistening of tomato purée and a little oil on the top.

Cover the dish and cook in an oven at medium temperature for approximately 30 minutes.

Arroz con P

115 Paella Espagñol

SPAIN

SERVES SIX

1 cup uncooked rice
½ a small raw chicken
1 small cooked lobster
1 lb. prawns
½ lb. fried scallops
1 small tin artichoke hearts
½ lb. peas
2 medium tomatoes
1 small onion
1 small clove garlic, finely chopped
pimiento
3 cups chicken broth
3 tablespoons olive oil
powdered saffron
salt

Shell the prawns and remove the lobster flesh from the shell. Cut up the chicken, brown it in a little oil, then simmer it in 3 cups of water for 20 minutes.

Meanwhile, cook the onion gently in the oil used for the chicken. Add the garlic, then the tomatoes, and cook until tender. Add the rice and mix well. Arrange the peas, scallops, lobster, prawns, chicken and artichokes attractively on top of the rice, then add 2 cups of boiling chicken broth. When the rice boils, add salt to taste, and the saffron (blended with a little broth). Place the pimiento on top and continue to cook until the rice is tender (approximately 15–20 minutes in all). The Paella may be cooked in the oven for the last 5 minutes.

116 Spanish Rice

SPAIN

SERVES SIX

1½ cups uncooked rice
4 oz. minced pork
4 oz. minced steak
4 oz. bacon, diced
8 oz. tomatoes, peeled and sliced
1 onion, sliced
1 red pepper, diced
1 green pepper, diced
2 cloves garlic, crushed
2 tablespoons tomato paste
1 cup chicken stock
8 cups water
2 oz. oil
salt and pepper

Cook the rice in boiling, salted water for approximately 15 minutes, then strain. Heat the oil in a pan and fry all the other ingredients for 5 minutes. Mix with the rice and add the chicken stock. Transfer the mixture to an oven-dish, and bake in an oven at moderate temperature for 20 minutes. If the dish becomes dry, add a little stock or water.

117 Spanish Chicken

SPAIN

SERVES SIX TO EIGHT

1 cup uncooked rice
1 chicken (4-5 lb.), cut up
1 cup cooked peas, drained
1 large can tomatoes
½ cup finely-chopped onions
½ cup finely-chopped green peppers
2 whole cloves
1 clove garlic, crushed
¼ cup chopped pimiento
1 cup black olives, cut into large pieces
2½ cups juice drained from the tomatoes (plus water)
2 tablespoons olive oil
¼ cup olive oil
bay leaf
pinch oregano
1 dessertspoon salt
½ teaspoon pepper

In a large pan, brown the chicken in ¼ cup hot olive oil. Add the tomatoes, onion, green peppers, clove garlic, bay leaf, cloves, oregano, salt and pepper. Simmer for 5 minutes, then pour into a large casserole.

In the same pan, cook the rice in 2 tablespoons of oil, stirring until golden. Add, with the tomato juice, to the chicken. Bake for 1½ hours in an oven at moderate temperature, until the chicken is tender and the rice is cooked, tossing once or twice. Toss in the olives, pimiento and peas, then bake for a further 15 minutes.

118 Paella Valenciana

SPAIN

SERVES FOUR

13 oz. uncooked rice
1 chicken (medium-size)
8 crayfish
8 small pieces of eel
12 snails
lean bacon
1 small tomato, peeled
2 globe artichokes
french beans
1 clove garlic, chopped
2 pints water
2½ oz. oil
saffron
1 teaspoon ground red paprika

First, cut the chicken into 14–16 pieces, and salt. Put 2½ oz. oil into a medium-sized casserole and, when very hot, put the chicken into it. Fry lightly, with some pieces of lean bacon, for 5 minutes. Add the tomato (cut into pieces), the garlic, french beans and globe artichokes. Add the paprika and rice (all well fried) and 2 pints hot water. When the water is boiling, add a little saffron, the pieces of eel, the snails and salt to taste.

When the rice is half-cooked, add 2 crayfish per person.

The rice should be cooked on a medium heat for 2–3 minutes. Reduce the heat and cook for another 10–12 minutes. It can then be put in the oven to dry.

119 Rice with Green Peppers and Cheese

SPAIN

SERVES SIX
2 cups uncooked rice
4 oz. grated parmesan cheese
1 onion, chopped
2 green peppers, cut into thick slices
1 clove garlic, crushed
1 cup cream
4 cups chicken stock
4 oz. butter
salt and pepper

Cook the onion and garlic in 2 oz. butter until the onion is transparent. Add the rice and cook, stirring, until it begins to turn golden. Add the stock and simmer gently until the rice is barely tender (approximately 15 minutes). In a buttered casserole-dish, lightly fork in half the rice, arrange half the pepper rings on it, and sprinkle with half the cheese. Top with the remaining rice, pepper rings and cheese. Dot with the remainder of the butter, pour over the cream, and bake in a hot oven for 15–20 minutes.

Serve as a light entrée or luncheon dish, or as an accompaniment to grills.

120 Sarma (Spicy Rice Stuffed Cabbage Leaves)

YUGOSLAVIA

¾ cup ready-cooked rice
1 lb. minced steak
1 cabbage
1 onion, chopped
cornflour
1 cup stock
olive oil
2–3 bay leaves
1 teaspoon crushed coriander seeds

Cut the leaves carefully from the cabbage and select the most suitable for rolling the meat mixture in. Trim the stems, then put them in boiling water and cook for 7 minutes. Drain thoroughly.

Fry the onion in a little olive oil until soft, then put into a bowl with the minced steak and the rice. Season with salt and pepper, add the coriander seeds and mix well. Put a good tablespoon of this mixture onto each cabbage leaf, roll up neatly and tie with thread. Place the rolls in a casserole-dish with the bay leaves and pour over the stock. Cover and simmer gently in the oven for 45 minutes. Lift out the stuffed cabbage leaves carefully, remove the thread and arrange on a dish. Keep the cabbage rolls hot while the stock is thickened to a sauce on the stove, using a little blended cornflour. Pour the sauce over the cabbage rolls and sprinkle them with finely-chopped parsley.

Serve with thick slices of crusty french bread.

121 Lovački Djuveč (Hunter's Stew)

YUGOSLAVIA

SERVES FOUR TO SIX

1 cup ready-cooked rice
3 lb. chuck steak, cut into 2″ cubes
8 slices bacon, chopped
1 cup sliced carrots
1½ cups finely-chopped onions
2 medium-size green peppers
1 teaspoon finely-chopped garlic
1¼ cups beef stock
2 cups water
¼ cup wine vinegar
salt
freshly-ground black pepper

Cook the bacon over medium heat in a large saucepan for 6–8 minutes, until it has rendered most of its fat and is slightly crisp. Remove the bacon, pour off most of the fat and add the onions. Cook them for 3–4 minutes, until they are slightly translucent, stirring occasionally. Add the garlic and carrots and cook for 5–6 minutes longer. Return the bacon to the saucepan, stir in the water and vinegar and add the beef cubes, salt and black pepper. Reduce the heat to its lowest point and simmer, covered, for approximately 1 hour, until the beef is tender.

Remove the seeds from the peppers and slice them into thin strips. Gradually add the rice to the saucepan, then the strips of peppers and 1 cup of the beef stock. Bring the liquid to the boil, then reduce the heat to low, cover and simmer for 20 minutes, until the rice is tender. Taste for seasoning. If the rice becomes too dry, add the remainder of the beef stock.

Serve with a mixed green salad.

Sarma (Spicy Rice Stuffed Cabbage Leaves)

American and West Indian Dishes

122 Brazilian Rice

BRAZIL

1 cup uncooked rice
1 cup peeled tomatoes
1 onion, chopped
1 1/4 cups water
1 tablespoon oil
1 teaspoon salt
1/2 teaspoon black pepper

Using a heavy stew-pan with a well-fitting lid, heat the oil and brown the onion well. Add the tomatoes, heat, and add the rice, stirring to prevent sticking. Add the salt and pepper. When the rice begins to swell, add the water (heated to boiling point). Do not stir. When all is boiling, cover the pan and lower the heat. Simmer gently for 30 minutes until the liquid is absorbed and the rice is tender.

123 Cuban Picadillo

CUBA

SERVES TWELVE

Cuban Fluffy Rice
1 1/2 lb. round beef
1 lb. lamb
1/2 lb. pork
3 hard-boiled eggs
6 large tomatoes, chopped
6 large onions, chopped
1 large green pepper, chopped
3 pimientos
12 large green olives, sliced
6 cloves garlic, minced
3 tablespoons chopped parsley
1 cup whole blanched almonds
1 cup seedless raisins
2 cups claret
1/2 cup butter
juice of 3 lemons
3 bay leaves, crumbled
1 teaspoon oregano
2 teaspoons saffron powder
2 tablespoons pepperoni
3 tablespoons capers
1 teaspoon powdered cummin seed
salt

Cuban Fluffy Rice

2 lb. uncooked rice
1/2 cup butter
1 tablespoon salt

Finely mince together the beef, lamb and pork, mixing the meat well together. In a large saucepan, lightly sauté the tomatoes, green pepper, onion, pimiento and garlic cloves in the butter, then remove them. Put a layer of the mixed meats in the bottom of the saucepan and sprinkle with salt. Add several spoons of the tomato mixture, a little lemon juice, some of the blanched almonds and the raisins, a few sliced green olives (with juice) and some of the pepperoni. Then add a pinch of saffron powder and sprinkle some capers (with juice) and chopped parsley, then a pinch of each of the crumbled bay leaves, powdered cummin seed and powdered oregano. Now add another layer of the meats and repeat the above procedure until all the ingredients are used. Pour slowly over all, the claret and enough water to come just to the brim of the meat mixture. Leave the pot uncovered. Simmer slowly over a low heat for 2 hours, stirring occasionally.

Serve hot over the Cuban Fluffy Rice.

Cuban Fluffy Rice
Put the washed rice into a large saucepan, cover with boiling water and add the salt. Bring the water to the boil again and cover the pot. Lower the heat and steam until the grains are tender (testing between fingers). Empty into a large colander and rinse until the water is clear. Into a separate pot, put half the butter, then add the drained rice with the remainder of the butter on top. Lay a piece of wet, brown wrapping paper over the rice and put the pot into a slow oven. When the paper is dry, put the rice on top of the stove at the lowest possible heat. Each grain should be distinct and separate.

124 Ham'n'Pineapple Quick Dish

HAWAII

SERVES SIX

4 cups ready-cooked rice
1 ½ cups diced cooked ham
6 pineapple slices
1 onion, finely chopped
1 cup diced green pepper
1 tablespoon brown sugar
½ cup milk
½ cup water
2 tablespoons melted butter
1 tablespoon french mustard
½ teaspoon salt
pepper
slices of red pepper (for garnish)
parsley sprigs (for garnish)

Cook the diced green pepper and the onion in the water until tender, then add the mustard, salt, pepper, rice, diced ham and milk. Simmer until the milk is almost absorbed then transfer to a shallow greased oven-ware dish. Arrange the pineapple slices on the top. Brush over with melted butter, sprinkle with the sugar and grill until the pineapple is browned.

Garnish with slices of red pepper and parsley sprigs.

125 Hawaiian Rice Salad

HAWAII

SERVES EIGHT TO TEN

2 cups ready-cooked rice
1 cup grated processed cheese
¾ cup diced pineapple
½ cup grated carrot
1 cucumber
½ cup mayonnaise

Toss the rice, pineapple, carrot and cheese together and turn into a salad bowl. Scrape the cucumber skin with a fork, then cut into thin slices and use to garnish. Serve with mayonnaise.

This is a basic recipe, to which other ingredients may be added according to your own choice. Half a cup of any of the following will blend well into the mixture:– olives, sultana grapes, walnuts, red pepper, chopped ham, dates, avocado, cold cooked broad beans.

126 Pineapple Rice Salad

HAWAII

SERVES SIX TO EIGHT

1 cup ready-cooked rice
¼ cup diced cheese
½ cup chopped pineapple (drained)
pineapple juice
lettuce leaves
1 green pepper, chopped
¼ cup chopped olives
½ cup raisins
salad dressing

Mix ½ cup rice with the pineapple juice and chill in the refrigerator. Mix together the remaining ½ cup rice, the raisins, chopped pineapple, pepper, olives, cheese and salad dressing. Decorate with wedges of pineapple, and sprinkle with the rice drained from the pineapple juice.

Hawaiian Rice Salad

127 Orange Rice with Bananas

SERVES FOUR

$\frac{3}{4}$ lb. uncooked long-grain rice
2 bananas, sliced
2 stalks celery, finely chopped
1 onion, finely chopped
2 cloves garlic, finely chopped
2 tablespoons finely-chopped parsley
$\frac{1}{2}$ pint chicken stock
6 tablespoons butter
juice of 1 orange
salt
freshly-ground black pepper

Melt 4 tablespoons butter and sauté the celery, onion and garlic until they are soft but not brown. Stir in the rice and fry, stirring continuously, until golden. Add the parsley, season to taste with the salt and black pepper, and add the orange juice and chicken stock. Cover and simmer for 12–15 minutes, until the rice is cooked.

Sauté the sliced bananas in 2 tablespoons butter until golden. Sprinkle with grated orange, and stir gently into the rice.

128 Banana Rice Fluff

HAWAII

3 cups ready-cooked long-grain rice
3 eggs
3 large bananas
6 tablespoons castor sugar
2 tablespoons slivered almonds
1 tablespoon lemon juice

Separate the egg-whites from the yolks and beat the whites until firm, but not dry. Place the yolks, sugar and lemon juice in a bowl and, without rinsing the egg-beaters, beat at the highest speed, adding the cut-up bananas. Beat until the mixture is thick and frothy. Fold into the egg-whites using a metal spoon. Put the rice into a buttered pie-dish, pour the beaten mixture over the rice and scatter the slivered almonds on top. Place in an oven at medium temperature for 12–15 minutes, until golden.

129 Rice and Banana Bake

HAWAII

½ cup uncooked rice
6 bananas
1 cup chopped marshmallows
apricot jam
1 pint milk

Without removing the skins, bake the bananas at a moderate temperature for 15 minutes in a dish with a little water. Cook the rice in milk until tender, then place in a greased oven-proof dish. Remove the skins from the bananas, slice and arrange them on top of the rice. Coat the bananas with apricot jam and sprinkle with chopped marshmallows. Re-heat in a hot oven, and serve immediately.

130 Rice with Chilli Peppers and Cheese

MEXICO

1 cup uncooked rice
8 oz. cheddar cheese, cut into small cubes
½ cup grated parmesan cheese
8 green and red pickled chilli peppers (drained, and cut into thin strips)
2 cups sour cream
butter
salt

Cook the rice in 8 cups of boiling, salted water for approximately 15 minutes, being careful not to over-cook, then drain. Combine the rice with the sour cream and season with salt. Spoon half this mixture into the bottom of a buttered casserole and sprinkle with the cheddar cheese and strips of chilli pepper. Top with the remaining rice mixture and dot with butter. Sprinkle with parmesan cheese. Pre-heat the oven to moderate temperature, and bake uncovered for 30 minutes. Serve immediately.

131 Crown of Rice with Avocado Sauce

MEXICO

SERVES FOUR TO SIX

1 ½ cups uncooked rice
1 onion, chopped finely
1 clove garlic, crushed
3 cups chicken stock
2 oz. butter
salt and freshly-ground pepper
Avocado Sauce

Avocado Sauce

2 avocados
3 tomatoes, peeled and diced
1 tablespoon finely-minced onion
1 tablespoon finely-chopped parsley
2 tablespoons olive oil
tabasco
salt

Heat the butter and sauté the onion and garlic. When the onion is transparent, add the rice and cook, stirring, until it begins to turn golden. Add the stock, salt and pepper and bring to the boil, then lower the heat, place the lid on the pan and cook very gently for approximately 20 minutes until the rice is tender. Spoon into a greased ring-tin and press firmly, to mould it into shape.

Turn out onto a flat serving-platter and spoon the Avocado Sauce into the centre. Garnish with the avocado slices. Serve the remaining Avocado Sauce separately.

Avocado Sauce

Peel the avocados and cut into dice (saving a few slices for garnish). Combine the tomatoes, onion, parsley, olive oil and diced avocados. Season well with salt and tabasco. Leave 1 avocado seed in the mixture to prevent the avocado discolouring.

132 Rice with Fried Bananas

MEXICO

SERVES SIX

2 cups uncooked short-grain rice
3 bananas, cut into quarters
1 onion, chopped
1 hot chilli, finely chopped
2 cloves garlic
chopped parsley
¼ cup flour
4 cups chicken stock
5 oz. butter
salt

Heat some of the butter and cook the garlic and onion until they begin to colour. Stir in the rice and chilli and cook until the rice is slightly golden. Stir in the chicken stock and seasonings. Cover and simmer very gently until the rice is tender and has absorbed the stock (approximately 20 minutes).

Lightly coat the bananas with flour and sauté in hot butter in a frying-pan until golden. Lightly fork the rice onto a hot platter in a high mound and top with finely-chopped parsley. Surround the rice with fried bananas and serve with grilled lamb chops or other meat.

133 Huachinango Veracruzano (Red Schnapper, Veracruz) MEXICO

Mexican Rice
1 red schnapper
bacon rashers
tomatoes, peeled and sliced
onions, chopped
chilli peppers, peeled and thinly sliced
green olives, chopped
pimiento strips
garlic, chopped
flour, sifted
bacon fat
capers
salt and pepper
wedges of lemon
watercress
parsley

Clean, wash and scale a large, fresh red schnapper. Stuff the inside with the Mexican Rice and spread the outside thickly with bacon fat. Pat on sifted flour to make a thin coat. Put the fish into an uncovered baking-dish, on several strips of bacon, but use no water. Make a sauce of the tomatoes, onions, garlic and chilli peppers. Put this over and around the fish and cook for 30 minutes. Sprinkle on the chopped green olives, salt and pepper. Return to the oven for 15 minutes (350°).

Serve with the wedges of lemon, strips of pimiento, capers, parsley and watercress. Allow ½ lb. per person.

Mexican Rice

3 cups uncooked rice
2 cups consommé (or strained stock)
few celery stalks
4 tomatoes
1 onion, chopped finely
1 green pepper
1 clove garlic
oregano
2 teaspoons chilli powder
paprika
salt and pepper

Sauté the rice in olive oil in a large saucepan. Keep stirring until the rice is quite brown. Skin the tomatoes and add them, together with the garlic, pepper and celery. Sprinkle the chilli powder on the rice, then add the consommé and 2 cups water. Boil fast at first, then reduce the heat and simmer for 20 minutes, until the rice has absorbed the moisture. Stuff the fish with the aromatic rice.

134 Red Mexican Rice MEXICO

2 cups uncooked rice
¼ medium cabbage, shredded finely
3 stalks celery, shredded finely
3 medium onions
½ green pepper, sliced finely
3 cloves garlic, crushed
4 cups chicken stock
1 oz. butter
3 tablespoons peanut oil
2 tablespoons soy sauce
¼ teaspoon chilli powder
2 teaspoons salt
pepper
shelled prawns and fried eggs (for garnish)

Chop 1 onion finely and thinly-slice the others. Heat the butter and fry the garlic. Add the chopped onion, sauté for 1 minute and sprinkle in the rice and cook, stirring, for 2 minutes. Spoon into an oven-proof dish and pour the boiling chicken stock over the mixture. Cover and cook in a hot oven for approximately 25 minutes until the rice is tender and dry.

Heat the peanut oil in a pan and fry the onion rings until well-browned, then remove. Add the cabbage and fry, stirring, for 5 minutes, then remove. Add the cooked rice, celery and pepper and fry, stirring, until golden. Add the chilli powder, salt and pepper and return the cabbage and onions to the mixture. Fry, stirring, until well heated through. Sprinkle soy sauce over and stir lightly to mix evenly.

Serve hot, garnished with prawns and fried eggs.

Avocado Rice Salad
(Recipe No. 137)

135 New Mexican Rice

1 ½ cups uncooked rice
1 cup green peas
1 cup diced carrots
2 tomatoes, peeled and diced
1 onion, finely chopped
1 red pepper, finely chopped
2 cloves garlic, crushed
4 cups beef stock
4 tablespoons olive oil
¼ teaspoon turmeric

Heat the oil in a heavy saucepan and fry the rice, stirring constantly, until the grains begin to brown. Place the rice to one side and add the garlic. When it is slightly brown, stir the garlic into the rice. Repeat this procedure with the onion, red pepper and tomatoes. Then add the beef stock, turmeric, peas and carrots. Cover and cook slowly for approximately 20 minutes, until the rice is tender and the liquid absorbed. If necessary, add a little more stock. Serve hot.

136 Chicken Supreme Rice Ring

U.S.A.

SERVES EIGHT

Rice Ring
2 cups diced cooked chicken
2 hard-boiled eggs, sliced
2 small carrots, diced
2 small onions, sliced
2 sprigs parsley
1/4 cup flour
1/2 cup heavy cream
2 cups chicken broth
1/4 cup butter
1/4 bay leaf
8 peppercorns
salt and pepper

Rice Ring

7 cups ready-cooked rice (hot)
1/2 cup grated cheese
2 tablespoons butter

Add the onions, carrots, bay leaf, peppercorns and parsley to the broth. Simmer for approximately 10 minutes, then strain. Melt the butter in a saucepan and stir in the flour. Add the broth, stirring constantly until smooth. Then add the cream and cook until thickened, stirring frequently. Fold in the chicken and the eggs and heat thoroughly. Add salt and pepper to taste.

Loosen the edges of the Rice Ring with a spatula, invert onto a platter and fill the centre with the creamed chicken.

Garnish with parsley, pimiento and additional sliced eggs.

Rice Ring

Add the cheese and butter to the rice and toss lightly with a fork until the cheese and butter are melted. Pack the rice lightly into a buttered ring-mould (8″ x 8½″). Cover with waxed paper. Set in a pan of hot water and keep warm until ready to use.

137 Avocado Rice Salad

U.S.A.

SERVES FOUR TO SIX

3 cups ready-cooked rice
1 avocado, sliced
½ cup diced cooked carrot
1 cup cold cooked peas
1 kernel corn (cooked)
gherkins, chopped
tomatoes, cut into quarters
½ cup chopped onion
¾ cup french dressing

Lightly toss all the ingredients together in a bowl. Serve chilled when the french dressing is thoroughly absorbed. Top off with the sliced avocado, gherkins and tomatoes.

For a really special rice salad, add extra ingredients to taste, and arrange layer by layer in a glass bowl. *(Illustration page 109).*

138 Cheese and Tuna Rice

U.S.A.

SERVES EIGHT

1 ¾ cups uncooked rice
1 can (6½ oz.) tuna
8 oz. shredded cheddar cheese
¼ cup chopped celery
1 tablespoon chopped onion
¼ cup chopped green pepper
2 tablespoons flour
1 ¼ cups milk
2½ pints boiling water
1 oz. butter
3 teaspoons salt
pinch of cayenne pepper

Cook the rice in the boiling water with the salt. Add the onion, celery and green pepper after 10 minutes. When the rice is cooked, drain and rinse. Place in a serving-dish, and keep hot.

Melt the butter in a saucepan, add the flour and cook for a few minutes. Stir in the milk gradually then bring to the boil. Add the shredded cheese and cayenne pepper. Continue cooking, stirring constantly, until the cheese has melted and the sauce is smooth. Add the tuna, and re-heat. Serve over the rice.

139 Rich Fish Gumbo Louisiana

U.S.A.

SERVES SIX

2 cups ready-cooked rice
2 oz. ham
2 lb. cod cutlets
1 ½ lb. tomatoes, peeled and chopped
1 onion, minced
2 pints boiling water
1 oz. ham fat (melted)
1 bay leaf, powdered
½ teaspoon powdered thyme
1 teaspoon salt
¼ teaspoon pepper

Heat the fat in a large saucepan. Add the fish and ham, cover and cook gently for 5–10 minutes. Remove the bones and skin from the fish, then return to the pan with the onion, pepper, salt, thyme, bay leaf and tomatoes. Add the water, then re-cover and allow to simmer for 1½–2 hours.

Serve in soup bowls with the hot rice separately.

Cheese and Tuna

140 Rice Ring Rio Grande

U.S.A.

SERVES SIX TO EIGHT

2 cups ready-cooked rice
1 lb. minced steak
6 frankfurts
grated parmesan cheese
½ lb. green peas (shelled)
1 can tomato soup
2 onions, chopped
½ green pepper, chopped
1 clove garlic, minced
1 cup consommé
butter
chilli powder
paprika
salt and pepper

Cut the frankfurts into rings, sauté in the butter and remove. In the same pan, sauté the onions, minced garlic and green pepper. Add the minced steak, the tomato soup, the seasonings and the consommé and, when heated through, add the cooked rice and mix lightly with a fork. Cook the peas quickly until they are bright green, then drain.

Oil a ring-mould and decorate the bottom with sliced frankfurts, putting small heaps of peas in-between. Add the rice mixture and keep over boiling water, then remove onto a round, hot platter. Sprinkle the grated parmesan cheese over all, and garnish with more peas and whole frankfurts.

141 Rice Griddle Cakes

U.S.A.

SERVES THREE

1 cup ready-cooked rice
1 egg, separated
½ cup self-raising flour
1 teaspoon sugar
¼ cup milk (plus additional milk)
1 teaspoon melted butter
¼ teaspoon salt

Gently heat the rice with the ¼ cup milk until it is soft, then add extra milk to make ¾ cup in all. Mix in the butter, the beaten egg-yolk, the sugar, salt and flour. Fold in the egg-white, beaten stiff. Bake the mixture on a greased griddle iron or in a fry-pan.

Serve with strawberry jam, maple syrup or honey.

Rice Ring Rio Grande

142 Ham Rolls

U.S.A.

SERVES FOUR

1 cup uncooked rice
8 thin slices of ham
½ cup chopped celery
1 small onion, chopped
½ red capsicum, chopped
3 cups boiling water
3 chicken cubes
8 teaspoons prepared mustard
salt and pepper

Place the rice, celery, onion, capsicum, chicken cubes, water, salt and pepper into a heavy-bottomed saucepan and bring to the boil. Then turn the heat down low, cover with the lid and simmer gently until all the liquid has been absorbed and the rice is tender. Allow to cool a little. Spread each ham slice with mustard. Divide the rice mixture into 8, form each into a roll, place one on each ham slice and roll up. Secure with a cocktail stick, then heat through in an oven at moderate temperature.

Serve with a tossed salad and crisp bread.

143 California Olive Rice

U.S.A.

1 ½ cups uncooked rice
2 cloves garlic, bruised
½ cup sliced black olives
2 cups tomato juice
2 cups beef stock
2 oz. butter
2 tablespoons olive oil
1 teaspoon chilli powder
½–1 teaspoon dill seeds, crushed
1 teaspoon salt

In a large frying-pan, brown the rice and garlic in the olive oil and butter. Add the tomato juice, stock, olives, chilli powder, salt and dill. Pour the mixture into a well-buttered baking-dish and bake, covered, in an oven at moderate temperature for 1 hour, until the rice is tender and the liquid has been thoroughly absorbed. Serve very hot.

144 Jambalaya

U.S.A.

1 cup uncooked medium-grain rice
1 cup cooked chicken, diced
1 cup cooked ham, diced
12 tiny pork sausages, cut into pieces
2½ cups canned tomatoes, undrained
1 cup finely-chopped onion
1 cup finely-chopped green pepper
2 cloves garlic, finely chopped
1 tablespoon chopped parsley
1 ½ cups chicken broth
2 tablespoons butter
¼ teaspoon chilli powder
½ teaspoon thyme
1 ½ teaspoons salt
¼ teaspoon freshly-ground pepper

Melt the butter in a large frying-pan and add the onion, green pepper and garlic. Cook slowly, stirring often, until the onion and pepper are tender. Add the chicken, ham and sausages and cook for 5 minutes longer. Add the tomatoes (with their liquid), the rice, broth, thyme, parsley, chilli, salt and pepper. Turn the mixture into a large casserole. Cover and bake in an oven of moderate temperature until the rice is tender (approximately 1¼ hours).

145 Seasoned Poultry with Rice

U.S.A.

½ cup uncooked rice
1 roasting chicken (4 lb.)
1 egg, well-beaten
⅓ cup minced celery
1 tablespoon minced onions
1 tablespoon minced parsley
½ teaspoon baking powder
1 cup toasted fine breadcrumbs
1 cup water
3 tablespoons butter
1 teaspoon thyme
½ teaspoon salt

Spread the rice in a shallow baking-pan and toast until golden-brown in a moderately-hot oven (400°) for approximately 20 minutes, shaking the pan occasionally so that the rice will brown evenly. Combine the rice, water and salt in a small saucepan, bring to the boil then lower the heat. Cover and cook slowly for approximately 14 minutes, until the rice is tender. Cook the onions, celery and parsley in the butter until soft. Remove from the heat and stir in the breadcrumbs, baking powder, thyme, salt, pepper, egg and rice. Toss lightly with a fork until combined. Fill the cavity of the chicken lightly and sew up the openings, then roast.

146 Lobster Newburg

U.S.A.

SERVES FOUR TO SIX
3 cups ready-cooked long-grain rice
1 lb. lobster meat
2 egg-yolks
3 tablespoons plain flour
2 cups white wine
1 glass sherry
1 cup cream
1 cup milk
3 tablespoons butter
1 teaspoon lemon juice
salt and pepper

Melt the butter in a pan, stir in the flour to make a roux, then add the milk, salt and pepper and half the cream, stirring until smooth. Pour in the well-beaten egg-yolks, the white wine, sherry and lemon juice. Do not boil. Add the lobster meat and the remainder of the cream. Heat through, and serve on the hot rice.

147 Jambalaya Lafitte

U.S.A.

SERVES SIX

1 cup uncooked rice
1 lb. raw shrimp, shelled
12 oysters
1 lb. raw ham
½ lb. breakfast sausages
2 cups canned consommé
1 cup peeled, chopped tomatoes
½ cup chopped onions
1 clove garlic, crushed
2 tablespoons chopped parsley
1 tablespoon flour
1 tablespoon oil
thyme
1 teaspoon pepperoni
paprika
salt and pepper

Heat the oil in a large saucepan. Add the onions and brown lightly, then add the flour, and brown. Add the ham (cut into small pieces), the skinned sausages, the shrimp and tomatoes. Simmer covered for ½ hour. Add the rice and the garlic, pepperoni, parsley, consommé and the seasonings. Cook covered until the rice is tender, then add the oysters and cook for a further 2 minutes.

Serve from a heated casserole or chafing-dish at the table.

148 Baked Rice Crab

U.S.A.

SERVES SIX TO EIGHT

1 cup ready-cooked rice
1 cup cooked crab meat, flaked
6 hard-boiled eggs, chopped
½ cup grated cheese
1 teaspoon minced onion
¼ teaspoon red pepper
1 ½ teaspoons chopped parsley
1 cup cream
1 ½ cups mayonnaise
½ teaspoon salt
⅛ teaspoon pepper

Combine all the ingredients (except the cheese). Place the mixture into buttered ramekins or shells and sprinkle with the grated cheese. Bake at 350° for 20 minutes.

Baked Rice Crab

149 New Rice and Tomato Soup

U.S.A.

SERVES FOUR TO SIX
1 cup ready-cooked rice
$^3/_4$ lb. onions, finely sliced
1 cup celery, sliced
2 cups milk
1 can (16 oz.) concentrated tomato soup

Using a large saucepan, bring the onions to the boil in a little salted water. Simmer the onions until tender, then add the celery, the milk and tomato soup to the cooked onions. Mix well and heat thoroughly, but do not allow to boil. Add the boiled rice to the hot soup and serve immediately.

Turkey with Oyster Rice Dressing

1 turkey (6–8 lb.)
1 tablespoon butter
1 tablespoon salt
pepper
Oyster Rice Dressing

Oyster Rice Dressing

2½ cups ready-cooked rice (in chicken stock)
1 pint oysters, well-drained
1 egg, well beaten
½ cup minced celery
¼ cup minced onions
1 ½ tablespoons minced parsley
1 ½ cups toasted breadcrumbs
¼ cup butter
1 ½ teaspoons poultry seasoning
salt and pepper

Mix the salt and pepper together and add the melted butter, then rub the turkey thoroughly inside and out. Stuff with 4 cups of Oyster Dressing, then close the opening with skewers and lace with string. (This keeps the bird in perfect shape while baking.) Place in a baking-pan and bake at 325° for approximately 2½ hours, until tender. Place the remaining Dressing in the baking-pan and bake covered for the last 30 minutes.

Oyster Rice Dressing

Cook the onions, celery and parsley in the butter until tender. Add the oysters and cook until the edges begin to curl, then remove from the heat. Stir in the remaining ingredients and toss lightly with a fork until combined. Fill the cavity of the turkey.

151 California Orange Rice with Seafood

U.S.A.

1 cup uncooked rice
seafood
asparagus spears
2 small onions, chopped
2 cups water
1 cup orange juice
1 teaspoon grated orange rind
3 oz. butter
½ teaspoon thyme
1 teaspoon salt

Melt the butter in a heavy saucepan and sauté the onions until they are soft. Add the orange juice, water, orange rind, salt and thyme. Bring to the boil and gradually add the rice. Stir, cover the pan, and simmer the rice for approximately 25 minutes, until it is tender but still firm.

Serve with fresh seafood and asparagus spears.

152 Grapefruit and Onion Salad

U.S.A.

SERVES FOUR TO SIX

2 cups ready-cooked rice
2 grapefruit, peeled and sliced
crisp lettuce leaves
2 crisp onions, thinly sliced
chopped parsley
french dressing

Arrange the lettuce leaves in a bowl and place the rice, grapefruit and onion on each leaf. Garnish with the chopped parsley and serve with french dressing.

Pineapple Rice Alaska (Recipe No. 160)

153 Ham with Fruit Rice Dressing

U.S.A.

SERVES SIX

2 cups ready-cooked rice (hot)
2 centre slices ham (½" thick)
1 small tart apple, diced
1 cup orange segments, diced
¼ cup seedless raisins
⅛ teaspoon ground cloves
2 tablespoons honey
3 tablespoons brown sugar
1 tablespoon butter

Combine the rice and butter and toss lightly with a fork until the butter is melted. Add the oranges, apples, raisins, brown sugar and cloves and spread in a baking-pan (10" x 6" x 2"). Cut the ham into 6 pieces and place over the dressing, then brush them with the honey. Cover and bake in an oven at moderate temperature (350°) for approximately 45 minutes, until the apples are tender and the ham is glazed.

154 Mexican Rice (Texas Style) U.S.A.

2 cups uncooked rice
1 onion, chopped
½ green pepper, chopped
1 garlic clove, minced
2 cups tomato or vegetable juice
2 cups canned consommé
1 cup olive oil
pinch of fresh chilli powder
celery salt
cayenne
paprika

Place 1 cup of olive oil in a casserole on top of the stove. Lightly sauté the rice until evenly golden-hued, stirring frequently. Add the onion, garlic clove and green pepper. Stir to prevent burning. Add the tomato juice and the consommé and season with the celery salt, paprika, cayenne and chilli powder. Bring to a brisk boil, then transfer to the oven and cook for a further 30 minutes at a low heat. The liquid should be absorbed and the rice dry and crisp.

Serve with half avocados on the shell, sprinkled with salt and lemon juice, and pieces of fried bacon or ham.

155 Jambalaya aux Ecrivisses à la Louisiane U.S.A.

SERVES EIGHT
3 cups ready-cooked white rice
2 lb. raw crayfish meat
leaves of 3 stalks celery, chopped
2 small onions, chopped
1 small green pepper, chopped
2 cloves garlic, chopped
1 medium can tomato sauce
olive oil
dash of cayenne
salt and pepper

Brown the onion, pepper, garlic and celery leaves in olive oil in a deep saucepan. Add the tomato sauce and seasonings. Simmer on a low heat to make a purée. After ½ hour, add the crayfish and boil for approximately 15 minutes. Add the cooked rice when the crayfish are about half-done. Cubed, cooked ham may be added.

156 Salmon and Rice Casserole

U.S.A.

SERVES FOUR TO SIX
3 cups ready-cooked rice
1 large tin red salmon
grated cheese
chopped onion
$\frac{1}{4}$ cup chopped parsley
$\frac{1}{4}$ pint cream
2 tablespoons butter
juice of $\frac{1}{2}$ lemon
salt
freshly-ground black pepper

Sauté the onion in the butter then mix well with all the other ingredients (except the cheese). Place the mixture in an oven-proof dish, top with the grated cheese and bake in an oven at a moderate temperature until heated through. Just before serving, brown the cheese under the griller.

Serve with a rich white sauce, to which 1 tablespoon of sherry has been added. Sprinkle with a pinch of nutmeg, and garnish with sliced hard-boiled eggs.

Creamy Rice Meringue (Recipe No. 161)

157 Turkey Casserole

U.S.A.

SERVES SIX

3 cups ready-cooked rice
2 cups cooked turkey, diced
6 slices bacon, diced
¼ lb. smoked cheese, cubed
2 tablespoons minced peppers
¼ cup flour
3 cups milk
paprika
1½ teaspoons salt
¼ teaspoon pepper

Cook the bacon until crisp, then measure off ¼ cup of the drippings. Drain the bacon. Stir the flour, salt and pepper into the bacon drippings, then add the milk, stirring until smooth. Cook until thickened, stirring occasionally. Add the cheese and stir until melted. Stir in the turkey and peppers and heat thoroughly, then fold in the rice and bacon. Pour the mixture into 6 individual 1-cup casseroles (or a 1½-quart casserole). Sprinkle with paprika. Bake in an oven at moderate temperature (350°) for 20–30 minutes, until thoroughly heated.

158 Seafood Rice Salad

U.S.A.

SERVES SIX TO EIGHT

2 cups ready-cooked rice
1 lb. prawns, shelled
1 lb. lobster
1 lb. crab meat
2 onions, chopped
1 green pepper, chopped
4 shallots, chopped
french dressing

Combine all the ingredients, and serve very cold on lettuce leaves. Garnish with lemon wedges.

159 Snowtop Peach Ricebake

U.S.A.

SERVES SIX

3 egg-whites
1 large can peach halves, drained
2 oz. glacé fruit
3 oz. sugar
brandy
½ cup cream

Creamed Rice

2 cups ready-cooked rice
3 egg-yolks, beaten
1 can condensed milk
1½ cups water
1 teaspoon lemon rind
1 teaspoon vanilla

Combine all the ingredients for the Creamed Rice (except the egg-yolks) and fill the mixture into an oven-ware dish. Bake in an oven at moderate temperature for 30 minutes until all the milk is absorbed. Stir with a fork several times whilst cooking. Add the beaten egg-yolks to the rice with the cream, then set aside and allow to cool slightly.

Chop the glacé fruit finely and soak for 1 hour in brandy. Place spoonfuls of the fruit on the rice, then cover each with peach halves. Beat the egg-whites until stiff, gradually add the sugar, and continue beating until the sugar is dissolved and the meringue is quite stiff. Spoon the meringue onto each peach-half and brown under a hot griller.

Serve hot or cold.

160 Pineapple-Rice Alaska

U.S.A.

SERVES SIX

3 cups ready-cooked rice
1 pineapple
1½ cups pineapple juice
1 can sweetened condensed milk
1 teaspoon vanilla
Meringue

Combine the rice with the condensed milk, the pineapple juice and the vanilla in the top of a double-saucepan. Cook over a low heat for 1 hour, until the mixture is thick and creamy. Place the mixture in an oven-proof serving-dish. Cut the pineapple into pieces, arrange them on top and cover with the Meringue. Place in a hot oven to brown the Meringue.

Meringue

3 egg-whites
3 tablespoons sugar

Beat the egg-whites until stiff, then gradually add the sugar. *(Illustration page 125).*

161 Creamy Rice Meringue

U.S.A.

SERVES SIX

2½ cups ready-cooked rice
3 egg-yolks
1 can condensed milk
1 tablespoon butter
1 dessertspoon lemon juice
1 tablespoon grated lemon rind
½ tablespoon vanilla essence
Meringue

Place the unopened can of condensed milk into a saucepan of water and boil for 30 minutes. (This caramelises the sugar in the milk and makes a butterscotch sauce.) Open the can and empty the contents into a bowl. Add the butter, beaten egg-yolks, lemon juice and rind, vanilla and rice. Mix thoroughly together and fill into a greased oven-proof dish. Spoon the Meringue on top of the Creamy Rice and brown lightly in a hot oven. Serve hot.

Meringue

3 egg-whites
1½ oz. sugar

Beat the egg-whites until stiff, then gradually add the sugar and continue beating until the sugar is dissolved and the Meringue stiff. *(Illustration page 129).*

Snowtop Peach Ricebake

162 Easter Bunny's Rice

U.S.A.

SERVES SIX TO EIGHT
2 cups ready-cooked rice
½ cup blanched, slivered almonds
¼ cup white sugar
¼ cup cherry brandy
2 cups whipped cream

Mix together the rice, cream, sugar and almonds, then chill thoroughly.

Serve with the cherry brandy poured over the top.

163 Rice and Banana Cream Pie

U.S.A.

SERVES SIX
2 cups ready-cooked rice
2 egg-yolks
2 large bananas, sliced
24 crackers, finely crushed
1/3 cup flour
1/2 cup sugar
2 cups milk
3 tablespoons butter
1 teaspoon vanilla
1/2 teaspoon salt
Meringue

Make a cracker pastry by binding the cracker crumbs with the melted butter. Line a greased deep 9" pie-dish with the pastry and bake in an oven for a few minutes at moderate temperature. Blend the flour, sugar and salt in the top of a double-boiler, then add half the milk, stirring until smooth before heating. Add the remainder of the milk while the mixture is cooking, stirring constantly until thick. Stir some of the hot mixture into the egg-yolks, which have been well-beaten. Pour this egg-yolk mixture back into the top of the double-boiler, add the rice and cook for a few minutes, stirring constantly. Add the vanilla, mix thoroughly, then cool.

Place some of the banana slices into the pastry shell, then add the rice cream filling. Top with the remainder of the banana slices and chill.

Spread the Meringue over the chilled filling and crust so that the entire top is covered, then bake in an oven at a moderate temperature until the Meringue is brown.

Meringue

2 egg-whites
1/4 cup sugar
1/2 teaspoon vanilla

Beat the egg-whites until they peak. Add the sugar and beat until the whites are stiff and shiny, then fold in the vanilla.

164 Colonial Rice

WEST INDIES

SERVES FOUR
4 cups ready-cooked rice
1 cup diced cooked meat or fish
2 bananas, sliced
2 slices pineapple
2 tablespoons chopped red pepper
1 tablespoon chopped fresh parsley
$\frac{1}{2}$ cup salted peanuts
2 cups light curry sauce

Place the meat, the bananas, diced pineapple and red pepper, parsley and peanuts into a pan, and toss over a low heat until heated through. Add the hot rice and mix thoroughly, then serve on a hot platter with the curry sauce poured over.

165 Creole Beef

WEST INDIES

1 cup uncooked rice
2 cups beef (cut into small pieces)
1 avocado, cut into small slices
2 tomatoes, sliced
1 white onion, sliced
2 cloves garlic, crushed
1 cup chopped parsley
½ cup olive oil
chilli powder
salt and pepper

Heat the oil in a casserole-dish, sauté the garlic then add salt, pepper and chilli powder and sauté the beef pieces. When the beef is thoroughly browned, add 2 cups of water and bring to a simmer, then add the rice. Cook slowly until all the liquid is absorbed by the rice and the rice is tender. Add the tomato, avocado and onion and cook slowly for a further 10 minutes.

Sprinkle with the parsley, and serve immediately.

166 Rice Topped Creole Cabbage

WEST INDIES

SERVES SIX TO EIGHT

3 cups ready-cooked rice
2 pork chops
½ cup concentrated mushroom soup
4–6 cups shredded green cabbage
4 tomatoes, peeled
1 cup sliced onion
1 dessertspoon lard
1 teaspoon paprika powder
2–3 teaspoons salt
¼ teaspoon pepper

Cut the meat into ½'' cubes and roll in seasoned flour. Heat the lard in a pan and brown the meat cubes briskly on all sides. Add the onions and cook them until they are tender. Add the tomatoes, shredded cabbage, mushroom soup, salt, pepper and paprika powder, cover the pan and cook until the cabbage is tender. If there is not enough juice from the tomatoes to prevent the mixture from sticking, add a small amount of water.

Spread the heated boiled rice on a platter and serve the creole cabbage mixture over the rice. Devilled eggs are an ideal accompaniment to be served with this dish.

167 Pilau of Seafood and Rice

WEST INDIES

SERVES SIX

1 cup uncooked rice
1 cup cooked prawns (or crab meat)
1 cup tomatoes
1 onion, chopped
1 cup oyster juice
1 cup vegetable juice
2 tablespoons butter
1 bay leaf, crumbled
½ teaspoon paprika
½ teaspoon salt

Cook the onion in butter until golden, then stir in the rice and cook until lightly coloured. Add the oyster and vegetable juices, the tomatoes, bay leaf, salt and paprika. Fold in the seafood, with a little cut-up boiled ham if desired. Cover the pan and bring to the boil, then reduce the heat and simmer for 25 minutes, until the rice is tender.

168 Pineapple Rice Pilau

WEST INDIES

SERVES FOUR TO SIX
1 ½ cups uncooked long-grain rice
1 small pineapple
¼ lb. brown sugar
1 ½ oz. almonds
1 ½ oz. cashew nuts
1 cup water
½ teaspoon ground coriander
½ teaspoon allspice

Simmer the sugar and water until syrupy. Add ¾ of the pineapple (cut into chunks) and the nuts. Cook for approximately 10 minutes until only a cup of syrup is left. Cook the rice for 7 minutes, then drain. Put the pineapple and nuts on top of a double-boiler, add the rice, and stir in the spices. Pour the syrup over and steam until the rice is tender.

Serve garnished with the remaining raw pineapple. This can be a dish on its own, or served with barbecued fish.

169 Riñones en Jerez con Arroz (Sherried Kidneys with Rice)

WEST INDIES

SERVES FOUR
3 cups ready-cooked rice
1 pair veal kidneys
1 onion, minced
creamed watercress
½ cup dry sherry
2 tablespoons olive oil
juice of 1 lemon

Sauté the onion, then add the sliced, cleaned kidneys and season. Add the sherry then cook over a low heat until the kidneys are tender.

Serve over the rice with the creamed watercress (add 1 cup chopped watercress, lightly sautéed in butter, to ½ cup undiluted cream of mushroom soup; season with a touch of grated mace).

170 Tortilla de Arroz (Rice Omelet)

WEST INDIES

SERVES FOUR TO SIX
1 cup ready-cooked rice
6 eggs, separated
5 tablespoons milk
2 tablespoons butter
powdered saffron
salt and pepper

Add the milk and a pinch of saffron to the egg-yolks, then beat with salt and pepper. Add the ready-cooked rice and mix thoroughly. Then fold in the stiffly-beaten egg whites. Grease an omelet-pan with butter, and heat. Pour in the egg mixture and cook on top of the stove until puffy. Put under a griller until the top is nicely browned.

Serve decorated with watercress and radish roses.

171 Di-ri et Djon-djon (Rice and Mushrooms)

WEST INDIES

SERVES EIGHT
2 cups uncooked rice
chopped ham
1 cup dry chinese mushrooms
4 cups water
crumbed thyme
marjoram
paprika
salt and pepper

Add 2 cups water to the mushrooms and bring to the boil. Remove from the stove and allow to steep, covered. Strain the mushrooms and press them with your fingers. Add the black liquid so obtained to the first cooking water. Chop the strained mushrooms and add to them the remaining 2 cups of clear water, with a spoon of bacon drippings, some chopped ham, crumbled thyme, salt, pepper, paprika and marjoram. Add the black water, then the washed rice. Start off at a high heat until it boils. Reduce to a simmer and cook for approximately 30 minutes, covered.

Pineapple Rice Pilau

172 Arroz Verde (Green Rice)

WEST INDIES

SERVES SIX

2½ cups ready-cooked white rice
1 cup crushed fried bacon
2 eggs, beaten
1 cup grated parmesan cheese
1 green pepper, shredded
2 cloves garlic, chopped
1 cup parsley and chives, chopped
1 cup milk
½ cup olive oil
1 teaspoon salt
¼ teaspoon pepper

Mix the rice with the seasonings. Sauté the green pepper and garlic in the oil then pour the pepper and oil over the rice. Add the parsley and chives. Beat the milk and eggs together, then mix with the rice. Place the mixture in a greased baking-dish and top with the grated cheese and bacon. Bake at 350° for 30 minutes until the egg mixture is set and the top is light brown.

Chopped watercress, young green spinach leaves or green onion tops may be used with the parsley and chives, all chopped together to achieve a brilliant green rice dish.

173 Creole Steak with Savoury Rice

WEST INDIES

Savoury Rice
1 lb. chuck steak, cut into strips
1 medium carrot, cut into strips
2 stalks celery, cut into strips
1 green pepper, cut into strips
1 red pepper, cut into strips
6 shallots, cut into strips
2 tablespoons flour
¼ cup sultanas
¼ cup raisins
1 cup stock
2 oz. butter
½ teaspoon mustard
pinch ground cloves
¼ teaspoon ground ginger
pinch nutmeg
1 teaspoon salt
freshly-ground black pepper

Mix together the flour, salt and pepper, then roll the meat into this seasoned flour. Melt the butter, add the meat and brown well. Stir in the other ingredients and mix thoroughly. Cover and cook gently until tender.

Serve with the Savoury Rice, and garnish with parsley.

Savoury Rice

2 cups ready-cooked rice
1 tablespoon finely-chopped green peppers
2 tablespoons finely-chopped red peppers
1 tablespoon chopped parsley
1 tablespoon butter
cayenne pepper

Mix together all the ingredients, and stir over a low heat until the butter melts. Dip a mould (or egg-cup) into the cold water and fill it with rice. Turn out, and repeat until all the rice is used.

Eastern Rice Dishes

Considering the fantastic variety of Eastern dishes, it comes as a shock to realize that there are comparatively few recipes which include rice as an ingredient in the dish. Rice is the traditional staple diet of most of the Eastern countries and this traditional role may have inhibited the development of rice as a constituent of other dishes. Another reason may be the symbolism associated with rice in the East. Not only is it a universal symbol of fertility, in many places it is also a symbol of purity, and for this reason there is a high degree of resistance to the idea of blemishing its whiteness by the addition of other ingredients in its preparation. The principal exception is saffron, which is added to make golden rice for festive occasions, notably weddings.

I have heard people say that Fried Rice is not a Chinese dish at all, but this is not so. However, it is not esteemed by the Chinese as it is by many Western devotees of Chinese food.

There are enormous provincial variations in Chinese cooking, so much so that there are restaurants in Hong Kong specializing in Szechwan, Peking or Cantonese dishes.

Due to the Dutch influence, Indonesian cooking is frequently an amalgam of Western and Eastern dishes. Nasi Goreng, in its many variations, is perhaps the most familiar Indonesian dish. This is no more than the national version of Fried Rice—regarded by the Indonesians as a breakfast dish but much esteemed by adventurous Western palates as a main dish at other times of the day.

Curries and highly-spiced recipes are not exclusive to India, you will find versions of these dishes in most of the Middle East and South-East Asia. Curry powder is specified for reasons of convenience, but curry paste may be used. An expert in Eastern cooking might prefer to use the actual spice constituents of curry, but good quality powder or paste is very acceptable. The degree of 'hotness' is a matter for individual preference. As in India, you may have it hot, medium or mild. The accompaniments are of the greatest importance to a good curry dish. A range of side dishes should be selected to provide as much variety of taste and texture as possible to the dish. Beef Curry is included in this book, but of course, due to religious reasons, it cannot be regarded as a typical Indian dish.

Some adaption to all Eastern dishes is inevitable, if only to overcome the limitations of the Western kitchen, particularly in the availability of spices, but where this has been necessary care has been taken to ensure that the integrity of the dish and its essential character are maintained.

174 Fish and Rice Kedgeree

CEYLON

SERVES SIX

2 cups ready-cooked rice
2 cups fish
hard-boiled eggs
dried lentils
3 onions, sliced
1 clove garlic, minced
red pepper
lime juice
1 bay leaf
turmeric
cayenne
salt
peppercorns

Place the raw, firm, white fish in enough water to cover. Add salt, peppercorns, bay leaf, 1 sliced onion and lime juice. Simmer until just tender. Drain, cool, and remove the bay leaf and peppercorns. Flake the fish, but not finely. Brown the 2 remaining onions and garlic in butter with red pepper and a little turmeric. When the onions are soft, add the rice, the fish, salt and pepper to taste and a slight pinch of cayenne. Sauté until everything is lightly browned. Sliced hard-boiled eggs and dried lentils may be added at the last moment of cooking.

Serve with small bowls of fried, chopped onions, chopped crystallized ginger and pimiento.

175 Chicken Pilau

CEYLON

1 lb. uncooked long-grain rice
1 chicken
8 slices fried bacon
4 boiled eggs
¼ lb. onions, chopped
¼ lb. sultanas
2 oz. almonds (or peanuts)
¼ lb. butter
½ teaspoon curry powder
½ teaspoon powdered turmeric
¼ teaspoon cinnamon
1 teaspoon powdered cardamoms
salt and pepper

Put the chicken into a saucepan. Add sufficient water to cover it and boil gently until it is half-cooked. Remove the chicken and cut into neat pieces, then rub them with pepper and salt. Heat a little oil in a frying-pan, add the pieces and fry until they are a golden brown. Remove the chicken pieces from the frying-pan, then add the butter and fry half the onions together with the curry powder. When the onions are brown, put in the rice, together with the rest of the onions, cinnamon, turmeric and chicken stock. Cook the rice, adding water as the rice absorbs the liquid. Add the sultanas and cardamoms when the rice is half-cooked, mixing in the nuts as soon as it is taken off the heat.

When serving, arrange the rice neatly with the pieces of chicken mixed into it, and the bacon and eggs (cut in halves) arranged on top of the dish.

176 Ceylonese Curry

CEYLON

SERVES EIGHT

4 cups ready-cooked rice
2 lb. fresh prawns
1 cucumber, peeled, seeded and chopped finely
3 onions, sliced
2 cloves garlic, minced
½ cup white corn-meal
1 cup coconut milk
fresh lime juice
3 tablespoons curry powder
crushed canton ginger
minced fresh mint, added to butter

Steam the prawns for 10 minutes, then drain and peel them. Season the prawn liquid and cook with the shells, the onions, garlic, salt and peppercorns. When spicy, strain, and make a smooth sauce using the corn-meal and curry powder. Add the ginger, salt, cucumber and lime juice, then the prawns. The coconut milk should be added last and just heated through, but not boiled (to prevent curdling).

Serve the curried prawns on the hot, cooked rice, seasoned with ghee (rendered butter) and flavoured with mint.

Ceylonese Curry

177 Tuna with Ginger Rice

CHINA

SERVES FOUR

Ginger Rice
1 can (15 oz.) tuna
1 cup sliced celery
1 cup sliced french beans
1 medium onion, chopped
1 tablespoon cornflour
1 teaspoon sugar
1 ¼ cups water
2 oz. butter
1 teaspoon soy sauce
½ teaspoon salt

Blend the cornflour with a little water. Melt the butter in a frying-pan and fry the onion until tender. Add the celery, french beans, salt and remaining water. Bring to the boil, cover and simmer for 5 minutes. Add the cornflour, sugar and soy sauce and cook for 3 minutes longer, stirring constantly. Add the tuna (in chunks), undrained, and re-heat.

Serve over the hot Ginger Rice.

Ginger Rice
3 cups ready-cooked rice
1 teaspoon ground ginger

Heat the ready-cooked rice in a saucepan. When hot, sprinkle the ground ginger over the rice and mix through thoroughly.

178 Chicken and Almonds

CHINA

4 cups ready-cooked long-grain rice
1 lb. chicken breast
½ cup mushrooms
1 cup sliced green beans
½ cup celery
½ cup onions
1 clove garlic
2 tablespoons cornflour
almonds
1 tablespoon white wine
stock
oil
green ginger (1″)
3 tablespoons soy sauce

Dice the chicken and vegetables. Mix in a bowl the wine and the salt. Deep-fry the chicken in very hot oil (380°), drain and remove. Blanch the beans. Heat the pan and add 2 tablespoons oil, sauté the ginger and garlic and remove when brown. Then sauté the vegetables in this order—onion, mushrooms, beans, celery—and return the chicken to the pan. Make a sauce with 1 tablespoon cornflour and 2 cups stock and mix it into the chicken mixture. Cook for 2 minutes longer, adding the toasted almonds before serving. Surround with the hot plain rice.

179 Kowloon Savoury Rice

CHINA

4 cups ready-cooked rice
4 oz. diced pork
4 oz. diced bacon
4 oz. small prawns
½ cup chopped green beans
8 oz. mushrooms, sliced
1 small onion, diced
3 tablespoons oil
2 tablespoons soy sauce
2 teaspoons savory (spice)

Heat the oil in a large frying-pan and sauté the bacon, mushrooms, pork, prawns, onions, beans and savory together for 2 minutes. Remove them from the pan and sauté the rice until heated through. Return the vegetables to the pan and mix lightly through the rice. Add the soy sauce and season with salt and pepper. Cook for 5 minutes longer, stirring frequently.

Tuna with Ginger Rice

180 Yeong Jow Chow Fan (Yeong Jow Fried Rice)

CHINA

SERVES FOUR

3 cups ready-cooked rice (cold)
½ cup barbecued pork (or cooked ham), diced
cooked prawns, diced or whole
1 cup shredded chinese cabbage
¼ cup shallot tops, finely cut
2 tablespoons oil
2 dessertspoons soy sauce
salt

Heat the oil in a wok or frying-pan and add the prawns and salt. Toss and turn for 2 minutes until heated. Add the pork, shallots, chinese cabbage and the rice. Press the rice mixture gently into the pan and fry for a minute or two until the rice heats through. Mix rapidly for 5–7 minutes. Sprinkle with soy sauce and pile into a heated serving-bowl.

181 Fried Rice with Eggs

CHINA

SERVES FOUR

4 cups ready-cooked rice
½ cup cooked pork (diced)
3 eggs
4 shallots
oil
2 tablespoons soy sauce
1 teaspoon salt
¼ teaspoon pepper

Beat the eggs lightly in a bowl. Heat the oil to high heat (380°) in a large frying-pan, add the rice and cook for 2–3 minutes, stirring constantly to separate the grains and to remove any lumps. Stir in salt and pepper, shallots and pork, and mix thoroughly. Form a hollow in the centre of the rice and pour in the beaten eggs. Scramble the eggs gently until semi-cooked and then gently stir them into the surrounding rice and cook for 2 minutes longer. When properly cooked, the egg should appear as long, fairly-firm strands right through the rice. Sprinkle with the soy sauce in the last 30 seconds, and serve hot.

This dish may be prepared using diced salami as a substitute for, or in addition to, the cooked pork. If salami is used, the dish will have a spicier finish.

Yeong Jow Chow Fan (Yeong Jow Fried Rice)

182 Soy Steak Supreme

CHINA

4 cups ready-cooked long-grain rice
1 lb. steak
1 cup green peas (and juice)
1 large onion, finely chopped
1 clove garlic
1 tablespoon sugar
oil
1 teaspoon ginger juice
3 tablespoons soy sauce
salt and pepper

Chop the steak into thin strips, then marinate in a mixture of soy sauce, sugar, ginger juice, salt and pepper for at least 1 hour. Heat the frying-pan and add 1 tablespoon oil and the garlic. When the garlic browns, remove and then sauté the onion. Remove, and add a little more oil to the pan. Put in the steak and, when the meat changes colour, return the onion, cooked peas and juice to the mixture. Mix well, cover and simmer for 5 minutes.

Serve on a bed of the plain rice.

183 Sweet and Sour Pork

CHINA

4 cups ready-cooked long-grain rice
½ lb. pork, cubed
1 egg
½ cup pineapple pieces
2 stalks celery
1 carrot
1 large onion
1 green pepper
cornflour
sugar
oil
1 tablespoon soy sauce

Marinade the pork in a mixture of the soy sauce, sugar and salt for at least 1 hour. Break the egg over the pork and mix well. Roll each piece of pork in the cornflour and deep-fry in hot oil until almost cooked. Drain, and then re-fry. Parboil the vegetables. Make the Sweet-Sour Sauce and add to the vegetables, adding the pineapple pieces lastly. Pour over the pork and serve with the plain rice.

Sweet-Sour Sauce

2 tablespoons cornflour
3 tablespoons sugar
½ cup pineapple juice
2 teaspoons tomato sauce
½ cup vinegar
1 knob of ginger
salt

Combine all the ingredients (except the cornflour) and bring to the boil. Blend the cornflour with a little warm water, and then add. Cook for 1 minute, stirring all the time. Remove the knob of ginger, and mix the Sauce with the vegetables.

184 Heavenly Chicken with Rice

CHINA

SERVES FOUR TO FIVE

4 cups ready-cooked long-grain rice
8 chicken legs or chicken pieces
1 cup sliced french beans
1½ cups carrot and parsnip straws
2 large onions, chopped
1 tablespoon arrowroot
1 tablespoon sherry
2 cups chicken stock
3 tablespoons oil
1 tablespoon soy sauce

Place the chicken legs into a saucepan and add 1 cup water and seasoning, cover the saucepan and simmer. Remove the chicken when it is tender. Keep the liquid, measure, and make up to 2 cups. Heat the oil in a fry-pan to a high heat (380°). Sauté the onions until golden. Reduce the heat slightly and add the carrot, parsnip and beans and stir for 3–4 minutes. Cover, and reduce the heat to 280°, then cook until tender (approximately 5 minutes). Add the soy sauce, sherry, stock and arrowroot and stir until thickened. Transfer the chicken and sauce mixture to a serving-dish.

Serve with the rice. *(Illustration page 157).*

Soy Steak Supreme
Sweet and Sour Pork

185 Canton Fried Rice

CHINA

SERVES SIX

8 cups ready-cooked rice (at least 12 hours old)
4 oz. prawns, peeled
4 oz. ham, cut into $\frac{1}{4}$" strips
$\frac{1}{2}$ cup chopped onion
1 green pepper, finely sliced
$\frac{1}{4}$ cup chopped shallots
2 oz. walnuts
2 oz. blanched almonds
2 tablespoons raisins
4 tablespoons oil
2 tablespoons soy sauce

Bring the oil to a high heat (380°) in a large frying-pan, add the prawns, nuts, raisins, ham, onions, shallots and green pepper. Cook for 2 minutes, stirring all the time. Add the rice and soy sauce, continuing to stir in order to keep the grains separate, and cook for a further 2-3 minutes until very hot. Serve immediately.

186 Indian Chicken Curry

INDIA

SERVES SIX TO EIGHT

Indian Fried Rice
1 chicken ($3\frac{1}{2}$ lb.)
2 onions, finely chopped
2–3 cloves garlic
6 cloves
handful of parsley
2 cups water
$\frac{1}{2}$ cup oil
1 tablespoon sesame oil
juice of 1 lemon
4 cardamom pods
2 cinnamon sticks
1 dessertspoon green ginger
2 tablespoons curry powder
$\frac{1}{2}$ teaspoon turmeric
salt

Joint the chicken. Heat the oil and fry the onion, garlic and ginger until golden brown. Add the curry powder, the turmeric, parsley and spices and fry, stirring, for 2–3 minutes. Add the chicken and stir well to coat with the curry mixture, then add the water and simmer until the chicken is tender. Add the lemon juice just at the end.

Serve with the Indian Fried Rice.

Indian Fried Rice

4 cups uncooked rice
1 onion, chopped
4 cloves
7 cups boiling water
$\frac{1}{2}$ cup oil
1 tablespoon sesame oil
4 cardamom pods
2 cinnamon sticks
1 teaspoon caraway seeds

Heat the oils in a saucepan and brown the chopped onion. Add the rice and fry lightly for approximately 5 minutes. Add the spices and salt to taste. Add 7 cups of boiling water, reduce the heat, cover and simmer for 20 minutes until the water is absorbed.

CINNA

187 Devilled Grilled Spatchcocks with Simla Rice

INDIA

Simla Rice
spatchcocks (allow 1 per person)
1 dessertspoon sugar
2 oz. butter
2 tablespoons tomato ketchup
1 tablespoon mushroom ketchup
1 tablespoon Worcestershire Sauce
1 tablespoon fruit chutney
1 tablespoon soy sauce
dash tabasco or chilli sauce
½ teaspoon curry powder
1 teaspoon ginger
1 teaspoon mustard
1 dessertspoon salt
1 teaspoon pepper

Split the birds in half. Mix together the salt, sugar, pepper, ginger, mustard and curry powder and rub well into the surface of the birds. Leave for ½ hour. Melt the butter in a small saucepan and brush generously over the birds. Place them on the grill rack and grill slowly until brown and crisp, then remove the rack from the grill pan and place the birds on the bottom. Mix all the sauces together in the grill pan with the remaining butter and heat gently, spooning the mixture over the birds. Cook, basting frequently, until the birds are tender.

Arrange the birds on a serving-dish on top of the Simla Rice. Dilute the sauce remaining in the pan with a little hot water, and spoon over the chicken. Garnish with watercress or parsley.

Simla Rice
3 cups ready-cooked long-grain rice
1 onion, sliced finely
2 oz. butter
1 teaspoon turmeric
salt and pepper

Sauté the onion in the butter until golden brown. Stir in the turmeric, cook for 2 minutes, then lightly fork in the rice. Warm through and season with salt and pepper.

188 Marinated Beef Curry with Garden Rice

INDIA

SERVES FOUR TO SIX
Garden Rice
3 lb. blade-bone steak
1 green apple, diced
2 carrots, sliced
½ cup diced celery
1 onion, sliced
½ cup onion rings
2 oz. seasoned flour
1 cup vegetable stock
¼ pint vinegar (brown or white)
½ cup vegetable oil
3 tablespoons curry powder
salt and pepper

Trim and cut the meat into 2'' pieces. Prepare a marinade by combining the oil, vinegar, onion and curry powder. Add the meat to the marinade and allow it to stand for at least 3 hours. Stir the meat frequently. Remove the meat from the marinade and coat with seasoned flour. Heat 3 tablespoons of the marinade in a pan, add the meat and brown on all sides. Remove the meat and brown the vegetables in the same pan.

Combine the meat, vegetables, stock, salt, pepper and half the strained marinade in a large saucepan. Cover and simmer for 45–60 minutes until the meat is tender. Add the apple during the last 15 minutes of cooking.

Serve with the Garden Rice, minted lemon wedges, nuts, chutney, bananas and pears.

Garden Rice
4 cups ready-cooked rice (hot)
1 cup cooked peas
¼ cup finely-diced celery
½ cup finely-chopped shallots
2 tablespoons chopped mint
salt and pepper

Garden Rice
Combine all the ingredients and mix thoroughly.

Heavenly Chicken with Rice (Recipe No. 184)

Indian curries come in an unbelievable variety. Recipes for the above group appear throughout this section

189 Egg Curry

INDIA

3 cups ready-cooked long-grain rice
6 eggs
2 tablespoons sour cream (or yoghurt)
½ tablespoon curry powder
1 teaspoon sesame seeds

Hard-boil the eggs, slice in half cross-ways and remove the yolks. Mash the yolks with the curry powder, the sour cream and sesame seeds. Re-fill the whites of the eggs.

Serve cold, sprinkled with chilli powder if desired, on a bed of rice. *(Illustration above left)*.

190 Curry Balls

INDIA

6 oz. ready-cooked rice
8 oz. minced cold meat (raw or cooked)
1 egg, slightly beaten
breadcrumbs
fruit chutney
juice of ½ lemon
1 tablespoon curry powder
salt and pepper

Blend the meat and rice and mix in the curry powder, lemon juice and seasoning. Bind the mixture with a little of the beaten egg and firm into round patties or balls. Dip these in the remainder of the egg, then in the breadcrumbs, and fry in oil.

Served topped with fruit chutney.

191 Oriental Beef Curry and Rice

INDIA

SERVES SIX

3 cups ready-cooked rice
1 ½ lb. steak, cut into 1″ cubes
½ cup shredded cabbage
1 potato, diced
1 cup pineapple pieces
1 onion, chopped
1 red pepper, diced
2 shallots, chopped
2 cloves garlic, crushed
1 teaspoon chopped mint
½ cup water
4 tablespoons butter
1 ½ dessertspoons curry powder
pinch cayenne pepper
1 ½ teaspoons salt

Heat the butter in a pan and add the onion, garlic and curry powder. Fry until lightly browned. Add the shallots and red pepper and cook for 2–3 minutes longer, then add the meat, salt and cayenne. Cook over a low heat for 5 minutes, turning the meat pieces frequently to ensure that they brown evenly. Add the potato and cabbage. When the meat is half-cooked, add the pineapple and ½ cup water, cover and simmer for 1 hour until the meat is tender, adding more water if necessary. Just before serving, add the chopped mint.

Serve with the rice and chutney.

Sweet Curry (Illustration overleaf)

192 Sweet Curry

INDIA

3 cups ready-cooked long-grain rice
1 ½ lb. lamb or mutton
2 apples, diced
1 pear, diced
1 medium onion, chopped
1 tablespoon flour
2 tablespoons sultanas
2 cups water
1 tablespoon butter
1 tablespoon lemon juice
2½ tablespoons curry powder
1 teaspoon salt

Cut the lamb or mutton into ½'' cubes. Heat the butter in a saucepan, add the onion and meat and stir until light brown. Add the flour and curry powder and allow to brown. Add the apples, pears, sultanas, salt, water and lemon juice. Simmer for 1–1½ hours. Place in a dish to serve, and garnish with banana slices.

Serve with the hot rice. *(Illustration pages **160** and **161**).*

193 Chicken Curry with Yoghurt

INDIA

3 cups ready-cooked long-grain rice
1 chicken (4 lb.), cut into serving pieces
2 cooking apples, cut up
2 onions, sliced
desiccated coconut
1 cup white wine
½ pint yoghurt
butter (for frying)
2 tablespoons curry powder

Sauté the apples and onions in butter, add the curry powder and fry for a couple of minutes. Brown the chicken pieces with the onion and apple mixture. When brown, add the yoghurt, desiccated coconut and wine (the wine to cover the mixture). Slowly simmer until the chicken is tender. If you prefer a hotter curry, add more curry powder or chilli powder.

Serve with the hot rice.

194 Fruit Pork Curry and Rice

INDIA

SERVES SIX
3 cups ready-cooked rice (hot)
6 pork chops
½ lb. prunes (seeds out)
½ lb. dried apricots
1 large onion, sliced
1 clove garlic, crushed
1 cup flour, seasoned with salt and pepper
2 cups boiling water
4 tablespoons vegetable oil
3 tablespoons curry powder
salt and pepper

Combine 1 tablespoon curry powder with the seasoned flour and coat each pork chop thoroughly (save some for the sauce). Heat 3 tablespoons oil in a frying-pan, add the garlic and brown each chop. Place them in a shallow casserole-dish.

Pour the boiling water over the prunes and apricots and set aside. Heat 1 tablespoon oil in a pan and fry 2 tablespoons curry powder and the onions until brown, then add the apricots, prunes and water. Blend the remaining seasoned flour and curry mixture with a little water, and add to the sauce. Stir over a low heat until thickened and simmer for 15 minutes.

Pour the sauce over the chops, cover with a lid or foil and bake in an oven at moderate temperature for 35–40 minutes.

Serve on a bed of hot rice.

Chicken Curry with Yoghurt

195 Rajah Chicken Curry with Golden Rice

INDIA

SERVES FOUR TO FIVE

Golden Rice
1 chicken (3–4 lb.), cut into sections
1 cup sliced mushrooms
½ cup diced celery
½ cup diced onion
2 tablespoons plain flour
½ cup currants
¼ cup desiccated coconut
1 cup chicken broth
3 tablespoons oil
½ teaspoon ground ginger
2 tablespoons curry powder
salt and pepper

Sauté the onions and celery in hot oil until tender, then remove from the pan. Brown the chicken pieces in the same pan, with a little more oil if necessary. To the browned chicken, add the sautéed vegetables and chicken stock. Cover and simmer gently for 20 minutes. Add the mushrooms, curry powder, ginger, salt, pepper and flour (blended with a little water). Mix thoroughly and simmer for a further 10 minutes.

Serve the curry on a bed of the Golden Rice, and sprinkle with the currants and coconut.

This curry may be accompanied by the usual side dishes, e.g. cucumber, coconut, nuts.

Golden Rice

1 ½ cups uncooked long-grain rice
2 tablespoons butter (melted)
1 teaspoon powdered turmeric

Place the rice in a saucepan and add sufficient water to come 1'' above the level of the rice. Boil rapidly with the lid off until most of the water is absorbed. Reduce the heat at once to the lowest point, cover firmly with a lid and steam the rice for 15 minutes to complete cooking. Add the turmeric (blended with a little water) to the rice and blend thoroughly. Heat the butter in a pan, add the rice and sauté gently for 5 minutes, turning with a fork. Garnish with chopped parsley.

196 Seafood Rice Curry Salad

INDIA

SERVES FOUR

3 cups ready-cooked long-grain rice
1 lb. prawns, peeled
1 cup scallops
lettuce leaves
1 lb. tomatoes, chopped
1 red or green capsicum, chopped
¾ cup french dressing
1 tablespoon curry paste

Chop half the prawns and scallops into small pieces and mix thoroughly with the rice. Add the tomatoes and capsicum, and the curry paste mixed with the french dressing.

Line a salad bowl with lettuce leaves and fill with the mixture. Decorate the top of the salad with the remainder of the whole prawns and scallops.

Serve chilled. *(Illustration page 176).*

Rajah Chicken Curry with Golden

197 Fried Rice with Prawns

INDIA

3 cups ready-cooked rice
1 lb. prawns, peeled and deveined
2 teaspoons chopped onion
½ clove garlic, chopped
1 tablespoon tomato paste
2 teaspoons butter
½ teaspoon curry powder
cucumber (for garnish)

Fry the garlic in butter for a few moments, then add the prawns. Fry for a minute or two longer and stir in the curry powder, onion and tomato paste. Cook for another 3 minutes, add the cooked rice and stir until hot.

Serve decorated with slices of peeled raw cucumber.

198 Prawn (or Egg) Curry with Lemon Rice

INDIA

SERVES SIX

Lemon Rice
2 lb. prawns (or 9 hard-boiled eggs, shelled and cut in wedges)
½ cup diced celery
½ cup diced cucumber (seeds removed)
2 onions, sliced
¼ cup green pepper, sliced thinly
1 clove garlic, crushed
3 tablespoons flour
1 cup yoghurt
1 pint vegetable stock
3 tablespoons oil
2 tablespoons lemon juice
2 tablespoons curry powder
¼ teaspoon ground ginger
salt

Shell the prawns (or eggs) and set aside. Heat the oil in a heavy pan and add the onion, garlic, celery, green pepper, cucumber, ginger and curry powder. Fry until the vegetables are browned. Remove from the heat, sprinkle over the flour and stir in. Add the yoghurt and stock. Stir over the heat until thickened and smooth. Simmer for 10 minutes then add the prawns (or eggs) and continue cooking for a further 15 minutes. Finally, add the lemon juice.

Serve with the Lemon Rice, and nuts if desired.

Lemon Rice

4 cups ready-cooked rice
1 tablespoon vegetable oil
grated rind and juice of 1 lemon
salt and pepper

Combine the hot rice, lemon juice and rind, oil, salt and pepper and toss thoroughly together.

Fried Rice with Prawns

199 Kofta Curry with Cool Cucumber Rice

INDIA

1 cup ready-cooked rice
1 lb. minced steak
2 eggs, beaten
3 tomatoes, peeled and chopped
2 onions, finely chopped
1 clove garlic, crushed
1 tablespoon chopped parsley
dry breadcrumbs
½ oz. butter
juice of ½ lemon
2 dessertspoons curry powder
2 teaspoons powdered bombay duck
salt and pepper
Cool Cucumber Rice

Combine the minced steak, rice, 1 onion, garlic, 1 dessertspoon curry powder, 1 beaten egg, lemon juice and parsley. Season with salt and pepper. Mix well and form into small balls. Dip in the remaining egg and then roll in the breadcrumbs. Fry until golden.

Fry 1 onion and 1 dessertspoon curry powder in the butter until the onion is soft. Add the tomatoes and the bombay duck, then bring to the boil. Add the meat balls and simmer for 10 minutes.

Serve with the Cool Cucumber Rice.

Cool Cucumber Rice

2 cups ready-cooked rice
1 cucumber, diced
1 cup chopped celery
¼ cup diced capsicum
¾ cup french dressing
2 teaspoons powdered bombay duck
salt and pepper

Lightly toss all the ingredients together until the rice is coated with dressing.

200 Prawn Curry and Curried Rice

INDIA

SERVES SIX
Curried Rice
2 lb. prawns, shelled
2 onions, chopped
1 clove garlic, finely chopped
1 cup chopped green peppers
1 tablespoon dry sherry
2 cups water
2 tablespoons chutney
butter (for frying)
2 tablespoons curry powder
1 tablespoon Indian curry spice

Fry the onions, peppers, garlic, curry powder and curry spice in butter until the onions are golden. Add the water and chutney and simmer gently for ½ hour. Remove from the heat and cool slightly. Add the prawns and enough water to cover, plus the dry sherry. Place in the refrigerator over-night. Heat through before serving, but do not cook for too long as this will toughen the prawns. If you prefer a hotter curry, add a little chilli powder.

Serve with the Curried Rice and the usual curry accompaniments.

Curried Rice

1 cup uncooked rice
1 onion, chopped
1 cup chopped green peppers
½ cup chopped shallots
1 chicken stock cube
water, as required
2 tablespoons butter
2 teaspoons curry powder
salt and pepper

Sauté the onions in butter, add the rice and cook, stirring, until transparent. Add the curry powder, peppers and shallots, then stir. Dissolve the chicken cube in water and add until it covers the rice by ½″. Stirring frequently, cook until the rice is tender. The liquid should be completely absorbed. *(Illustration page 181)*.

Kofta Curry with Cool Cucumber Rice

201 Prawn Shashlik with Saffron Rice

INDONESIA

SERVES FOUR TO SIX

Saffron Rice
1 lb. raw prawns, peeled
1 teaspoon brown sugar
½ cup sherry
½ cup soy sauce

Thread the prawns onto metal skewers and marinate in the soy sauce, brown sugar and sherry mixture over-night. Grill under a low heat for approximately 7 minutes. Be careful not to over-cook as this toughens the prawns. Heat the remaining marinade for sauce.

Serve over the Saffron Rice.

Saffron Rice

4 cups uncooked rice
1 packet powdered saffron

Boil the rice in water with the powdered saffron. When cooked, drain, and keep hot with plenty of melted butter until ready to eat.

202 Nasi Gurih (Rice in Coconut)

INDONESIA

6 cups uncooked rice
2–4 cups finely-shredded chicken meat (raw or cooked)
½ teaspoon shrimp paste
4 medium onions, grated
2 cloves garlic, crushed
6 kemiri kernels
1 tablespoon coriander
½ teaspoon laos
1 teaspoon cummin
6 teaspoons salt
6 cups Santan

Pound together all the ingredients except the rice, Santan and the chicken. When they have been pounded to a fine paste, add them, with the shredded chicken, to the Santan. Wash the rice and mix it well with the other ingredients, then bring it quickly to the boil, stirring the liquid to prevent curdling. As soon as it boils, cover tightly, reduce the heat to the minimum and cook for ½–¾ hour, until the liquid is absorbed and the rice cooked right through.

Santan

2 cups desiccated coconut (or 1 grated coconut)
1 cup warm water

Place the coconut in a basin and place a fine mesh strainer over another basin. Moisten the coconut with a little water from the cup and squeeze the liquid out through the strainer. Add a further small amount of water to the first basin, return the coconut to that basin, and repeat the squeezing-soaking routine until the water is used up. By adding only sufficient water to moisten the coconut, the greatest possible amount of Santan is extracted from it.

203 Nasi Samin (Rice in Butter)

INDONESIA

3 cups uncooked rice
4 onions, sliced
1 small clove garlic, crushed
6 whole cloves
3 cups water
¼–½ lb. butter
10 cardamom seeds
½ teaspoon ground cinnamon
¼ teaspoon ground nutmeg

Fry the onion and spices in the oil. Add the water and bring to the boil. Then add the well-washed rice, mixing it well with the onions and spices. Cook over a low heat until the water is absorbed and the rice is cooked through (approximately ½–¾ hour).

Nasi Samin may be served as a dish on its own. The recipe can be varied by adding chicken meat when the rice is added. Cashews or peanuts can be added just prior to serving.

Prawn Shashlik with Saffron Rice

204 Nasi Kebuli Mafrum

INDONESIA

4 cups uncooked rice
1 lb. finely-minced steak or mutton
2 large onions, sliced
5–7 cloves garlic, crushed
6 cloves
¼ lb. almonds
¼ lb. sultanas
¼ lb. butter
10 cardamom seeds
½ teaspoon turmeric
1 2″-stick cinnamon
salt
1 teaspoon pepper

First make the MAFRUM by frying the meat in 1 tablespoon butter until it changes colour. Add the onions and half the garlic with ½ teaspoon pepper and salt to taste. Cook until the onion is soft, then set aside.

Fry the almonds and sultanas in a little oil until the almonds change colour, then add them to the meat.

For the KEBULI, bring 4 cups water to the boil and add the rice, cover and cook until a grain rubbed between the fingers has no hard core. Drain off any surplus water. Meanwhile pound the remainder of the garlic, and fry in the rest of the butter. Mix in with the rice, salt, ½ teaspoon pepper, cinnamon, cloves and cardamom. Close the lid tightly and simmer on low heat for approximately 1½ hours.

When the rice is done, serve on a large platter, garnished with the MAFRUM.

205 Nasi Goreng

INDONESIA

SERVES FOUR
1 cup uncooked rice
1½ lb. chicken
½ lb. prawns
4 fried eggs
8 cabbage leaves
½ cup celery
1 large onion
1 clove garlic
2 tablespoons sultanas
1½ cups chicken stock
3 tablespoons soy sauce
3 tablespoons oil
1 teaspoon mixed spice
1 teaspoon gourmet salt
salt

Remove the meat from the chicken and cut it into small pieces. Place the bones in a saucepan with water and salt and simmer for 2 hours (for stock). Slice the onion approximately ⅛″ thick, cut the rings in half and separate. Slice the cabbage into ¼″ slices and measure 2 cups. Slice the celery across the stick approximately ¼″ thick.

Heat the oil in a fry-pan to a high heat (380°) and sauté the garlic, which has been bruised and sprinkled with salt. Remove the garlic and fry the onions until well-browned and cooked, then remove. Sauté the cabbage for 1 minute, and remove. Fry the rice and celery until lightly browned. Reduce the heat to 260°, add the stock, gourmet salt, spice and chicken and simmer gently for 15 minutes until tender. Shell the prawns, chop to the same size as the chicken pieces and add them to the rice, with the soy sauce, spice, sultanas, gourmet salt, onions and cabbage. Continue to cook until the chicken and rice are tender. Place a fried egg on each serving.

Serve from the fry-pan or a large platter, with selected accompaniments (e.g. prawn or potato crisps, banana and pineapple fritters, rich fruit chutney).

Nasi G

206 **Nasi Goreng** (Alternative Recipe)

INDONESIA

SERVES FOUR

4 cups ready-cooked rice
1 cup cooked chicken
1 cup cooked pork
1 cup cooked prawns
4 eggs
1 cup chopped onion
½ cup chopped green pepper
½ cup raisins (soaked in brandy)
1 teaspoon curry powder
1 teaspoon powdered ginger
powdered chilli
salt and pepper

Sauté the onions and peppers in butter. Add the curry powder, ginger, chilli powder, salt and pepper and fry, stirring, for 2 minutes. Add the raisins and brandy, the pork, chicken and rice and heat through, finally adding the prawns. Fry the eggs and place them on top of the rice mixture.

Serve with soy sauce, sliced cucumber and sliced tomatoes.

207 **Nasi Briani Ikan** (Rice with Fish) INDONESIA

3 cups uncooked rice
1 lb. fish cutlets
2–3 medium tomatoes, sliced
1 stick celery
2 large onions
5 cloves garlic, crushed
2 oz. butter
1 tablespoon curry powder
10 cardamom seeds
¼ teaspoon turmeric

Fry the fish in butter in a large saucepan until it changes colour. Add the curry powder and fry for another 2–3 minutes. Next add the garlic and fry until it softens. Add the tomatoes, and the onions cut into thin rings. Add the salt, a little sugar and 2 cups water. Simmer until the liquid has reduced to about 2 tablespoons.

Bring 3 cups water to the boil and add the rice, cover, and cook until a grain rubbed between the fingers has no hard core. Drain off any surplus water.

In a large aluminium saucepan, melt the butter. Put ⅓ of the rice in a layer, then a layer of half the fish, another ⅓ of the rice, the remainder of the fish, and top with rice. Add a few dabs of butter, replace the lid and simmer for approximately 1½ hours.

208 **Lemper** (Rice Croquettes) INDONESIA

2 cups uncooked short-grain rice
½ lb. meat
2 medium onions, grated
2 cloves garlic, crushed
2½ cups Santan (see recipe page 170)
3 kemiri kernels
¼ teaspoon cummin
½ teaspoon coriander
¼ teaspoon laos
salt

Soak the rice in water for 1 hour and then steam until half-cooked. Put the Santan and a little salt in a saucepan and bring to the boil, stirring constantly. Slowly add 2 cups of the hot Santan to the rice, stirring briskly all the while. Now continue to steam the rice until it is cooked through.

Meanwhile mince the meat very finely. Grind together the onions, garlic, kemiri and spices, sauté the mixture for 2–3 minutes in a little hot oil, then add the meat. Add the remaining Santan and cook until all the ingredients are done and the mixture is fairly dry

Make small cylindrical balls of the rice mixture and put a spoonful of the meat inside each. Wrap in oiled foil and grill.

209 **Pah Jook** (Rice and Beans) KOREA

SERVES SIX
1 cup uncooked rice
1 cup kidney beans
1 onion
1 clove garlic
beef stock
2 cups water
2 tablespoons peanut oil
salt

Soak the beans over-night and then simmer with the onion, garlic and salt in the same water until soft enough to mash through a colander. This purée is then fried in the peanut oil. Wash the rice and cook in 2 cups of boiling, salted water, until the rice is tender and dry. Then mix the bean purée and the rice together with a little beef stock.

210 Curried Pineapple Rice Kebabs

MIDDLE EAST

Kebabs

1 lb. leg lamb, cut into $\frac{3}{4}''$ cubes
$\frac{1}{2}$ lb. ham, cut into $\frac{3}{4}''$ cubes
1 can (16 oz.) apricot halves (reserve syrup)
pineapple cubes
4 oz. mushrooms
6 small onions
2 capsicums, cut into cubes
2 tablespoons oil
1 dessertspoon curry powder

Combine the curry powder, oil and apricot syrup. Add the cubes of lamb and ham and allow to stand for 30 minutes in the marinade, turning occasionally. Thread the meat alternately with the fruit and vegetables on skewers until all the ingredients have been used. Cook under the grill, turning and brushing frequently with the remainder of the marinade.

Serve over hot Pineapple Rice.

Pineapple Rice

1 $\frac{1}{2}$ cups uncooked rice
$\frac{1}{2}$ cup undrained crushed pineapple
stock (or water)
1 dessertspoon curry powder
2 teaspoons toasted sesame seeds
1 teaspoon salt

Place the rice, salt, curry powder and crushed pineapple in a saucepan. Cover the rice with boiling stock to a depth of 1″ and boil rapidly, with the lid off, until steam holes appear in the rice. Lower the heat to the lowest point, put the lid on firmly, and leave for 20 minutes for the steam to complete the cooking. The rice should absorb all the moisture. Mix the toasted sesame seeds thoroughly through the rice.

Seafood Rice Curry Salad (Recipe No. 196)

211 Lamb Curry with Sweet Rice

MIDDLE EAST

SERVES FOUR

Sweet Rice
2 cups diced cold cooked lamb
1 large cooking apple, peeled and chopped
1 can artichoke hearts
2 onions, chopped
1 green pepper, chopped
1 clove garlic, crushed
2 whole cloves
1 tablespoon flour
½ cup seedless raisins
¼ cup shredded coconut
1 dessertspoon sour cream
½ cup red wine
1 cup consommé
1 tablespoon olive oil
juice and grated rind of 1 lemon
1 dessertspoon curry powder
pinch dried thyme
pinch marjoram
½ teaspoon salt

Sauté the apple, green pepper and onion with the garlic in olive oil until the onions are limp. Sprinkle in the flour, curry powder, salt and herbs. Mix well, stirring constantly, and cook for 5 minutes. Add the consommé, wine, raisins, cloves and lemon rind and juice, and simmer for 20 minutes. Add the lamb and shredded coconut and heat for 15 minutes. Just before serving, stir in the sour cream. Top with hot artichoke hearts.

Sweet Rice

6 cups ready-cooked rice
1 dessertspoon sugar
¼ cup sultanas
½ cup slivered almonds

Spread the rice on an oven-tray and heat in an oven at low temperature for 15 minutes. Turn into a serving-dish and toss lightly with the almonds, sultanas and sugar.

212 Sherkasiya (Circassian Chicken)

MIDDLE EAST

ready-cooked rice
1 chicken
2 onions, chopped
3 oz. almonds, shelled
3 oz. walnuts, shelled
3 oz. hazelnuts, shelled
butter
cayenne
paprika
salt

Boil the chicken until it is tender, cut it into 4 pieces, and arrange it in the centre of a dish of hot, boiled rice.

The following sauce is served with it. Pound the walnuts, almonds and hazelnuts in a mortar with the paprika, cayenne and salt. Fry the chopped onions in butter, and add the pounded nuts and a little of the chicken stock. When it is thick, pour it over the rice.

Lamb Curry
with Sweet

213 **Beriane** (Rice with Meat)

PAKISTAN

1 lb. uncooked long-grain rice
1 lb. meat (with or without bones)
1 large onion
1 clove garlic
10 cloves
¼ lb. almonds, peeled and chopped
¼ lb. yoghurt
¼ pint milk
4 oz. butter
1 large bay leaf
½ oz. coriander seeds
2 large cardamoms
½ teaspoon cummin seeds
1 oz. green ginger
small piece of cinnamon
pinch of saffron
2 teaspoons salt
8 seeds black pepper

Make a fine paste of the onion, garlic, green ginger, coriander seeds and salt, and mix with the chopped meat. Heat the butter in a frying-pan and add the cloves and cardamoms. When the cloves are fried, add the meat, yoghurt, cinnamon, cummin seeds, bay leaf and black pepper. Stir on a medium heat until the meat turns brown.

Add the rice (which should have been washed and soaked for 2 hours) with 1½ pints water, and stir until it boils. Cook on a medium heat for 30 minutes, and then add the saffron mixed with the milk and almonds. Continue to cook until the rice is tender.

214 Syrian Chicken and Rice

SYRIA

SERVES EIGHT TO TEN
1 lb. uncooked rice
1 fat chicken
1 lb. lamb
¼ lb. chick peas
1 lb. onions, chopped finely
4 cloves garlic, chopped finely
olive oil
paprika
parsley
salt and pepper

Brown the onions and garlic in olive oil in a large frying-pan. When golden, add the cut-up meat and chicken, and brown. Add the soaked chick peas. Season and cover just to the top with water or broth. Cook slowly for approximately 2 hours. Add the rice during the last 30 minutes, and cook until the rice has absorbed the liquid. Serve immediately.

215 Larp

THAILAND

1 cup ready-cooked rice
1 lb. minced meat
sugar
juice of 1 lemon
1 teaspoon chilli powder
salt

Using just enough oil to prevent burning, dry fry the rice until it is brown, and then grind it to a powder. Mix the lemon juice with the meat, and then drain the juices into a saucepan and boil. Add the meat to the saucepan with the salt, rice powder, sugar and chilli powder.

Serve Larp with fresh green vegetables (lettuce, cucumber, cabbage).

Prawn Curry and Curried Rice (Recipe No. 200)

Danish Almond Rice
Riz à la Dreux
Cuban Picadillo
Rice of the Ritz
Red Mexica
Czardaz Veal with Caraway Rice
en with Rice, Basque Style
Louisiane
Banana Rice Fluff
Risotto
Jambalaya
Salad Royale with Green Mayonnaise
Rum Baked Rice
Sherkasiya
Fish and Rice Kedgeree
New Mexican Rice
Bavarian Beef Crust Pie
Mexican Rice
Lattice Meat Pie
Paella Valenciana
Nasi Gurih
Prawn Shashlik with Saffron Rice
d Rice Crab
Tuna with Ginger Rice
Di
ice
d Fish Kedgeree
Beriane
Rice Biscuits
Cheese an
Rice with Fried Bananas
Rice Griddle Cakes
Portuguese Risotto with Mushrooms
Yeong Jow Fried Rice
Loganberry Applebake
Fruit Pork Curry
Risotto Milanese
Syrian Chicken and
Orange Rice with Bananas
Crown of Rice with Avoc
ux Herbes
Sasaties
cken and Almonds
Avocado Rice Salad
Letsho
Dutch Rice Curry Casserole
Danish Rice Pudding
Poulet a
Dutch Curry and Rice Soup
Briani Ikan
Paella Barcelona
Rice à la Grecque
Rice with Chilli
Kofta Curry with Cool Cucumber Rice
Risotto à la Norton
iz Indienne
Sweet and Sour Pork
Ceylone
Paella à la Catalana
Devilled Grilled Spatchcocks with Simla Rice
Pear
ce
Swedish
Osso Bucco
Dutch Oven Meat Balls with Chervil Rice
Nasi Kebuli Mafrum
Riso al Limo
nated Beef Curry with Garden Rice
Pineapple-Rice Alaska
English Rice Pudding
Salmon Cheese Casserole
Stuffed Edam Cheese
Chicken Curr
Tor
and Banana Cream Pie
Bee-Hive Bavarian
Brazilian Rice
e Salad
Poule-au-Pot
Arroz co
Suliman's Pilaff
Venetian Risotto
key with Oyster Rice Dressing
Rice Ring Rio Grande
Lobster Newburg
Rolls